88

FLAK & PAK

A Profile Special

by Peter Chamberlain and
Terry Gander

Edited by
Duncan Crow

Illustrations by
Terry Hadler

PROFILE PUBLICATIONS LTD
Windsor, Berks

Contents

The 88 — Flak and Pak

by Peter Chamberlain & T. J. Gander

ON 26th May 1941 Rommel wrote in his diary:

'In constructing our positions at Halfaya and on Hill 208 great skill was shown in building in batteries of 88 mm. guns for anti-tank work, so that with the barrels horizontal there was practically nothing to be seen above ground. I had great hopes of the effectiveness of this arrangement.'

Rommel's hopes were fully realized. During the frontier Battle of Sollum in early June 1941, 123 out of 238 available British tanks were destroyed by those well emplaced guns. There were only 13 dug in along the German positions, but they were able to pick off the British tanks at ranges well in excess of the light tank guns, and were also able to penetrate the thick armour of the Matilda, hitherto invulnerable to German anti-tank guns.

Thus one of the legends of the Second World War was born. The word soon spread that the Germans had a new secret weapon, a 'wonder gun' that could penetrate all Allied armour at ranges well over any other anti-tank gun in service. But like all such legends, the truth was that the 8.8 cm. (3.46″) Flak 18 and 36 guns used at Sollum should not have come as such a nasty surprise to the Allies, for the use of this anti-aircraft weapon as an anti-tank gun had been part of the German tactical repertoire since the Spanish Civil War. The B.E.F. had first experi-enced the '88' in combat at Arras in May 1940, but the fact seems to have escaped official notice. Indeed, the lineage of the Halfaya guns can be traced back to 1916.

GENERAL SURVEY

Early Development

By 1916 aircraft had begun to make a decided difference to the tactical situation on the battle-fields of the First World War. Used mainly for reconnaissance and artillery observation its employment was still in its infancy but already the first air-to-air combats had taken place and the ground forces were looking for some means of attacking enemy machines. On the German side there were many and varied lash-ups of existing field pieces that should not have been necessary since far-sighted German designers had been producing high angle guns for use against balloons since 1870. In 1906, Erhardt had mounted a 5 cm. BAK (Ballon Abwehr Kanone) on an armoured chassis, and Daimler followed in 1909 with a 5.7 cm. Flak (Flugzeugabwehr-kanone) on its 'Panzerkraftwagen'. Neither of these vehicles were taken into service but by 1914 a small German anti-aircraft arm equipped with only 18 guns was in being. Some of these guns were very limited in range as they were intended primarily for use against balloons, and their usual calibre was 7.7 cm., L/27. A demand for

An 8.8cm Pak 43/41 L71 ready for action. (Bundesarchiv).

3

more powerful weapons was made to industry and the first results were seen in 1916.

In that year two almost identical guns were produced by the armament giants of Krupps and Rheinmetall-Borsig. Both were designated Geschütze 8.8 cm. KwFlak or 8.8 cm. K.Zug Flak, and used a L/45 barrel. Rather unusual for their day was that they were highly mobile and designed from the outset for towing by motor tractors. Mounted on flat four wheeled trailers, the guns were stabilised in action by four outrigger arms (two a side) which were swung out in use. Sighting was usually by direct vision methods but by late 1918 rudimentary forms of centralised control were in use. Details of these two 8.8 cm. guns follow:—

Length of barrel (calibres)	45
Weight of shell	9.6 kg.
Muzzle velocity	785 metres/sec.
Maximum range	10,800 metres
Maximum height	6,850 metres
Weight in action	3,000 kg.
Weight in transit	7,300 kg.

The 1919 Versailles Treaty imposed stringent sanctions on the German armament firms. In particular Krupps were hit by the clause which prevented them from making guns below 17 cm. in calibre. As guns above this calibre were never in very great demand, Krupps cast around for some means of guarding their future interests in the field artillery market – hitherto their largest money-maker. By 1921 an arrangement had been made with the Swedish firm of Bofors. By the agreement, Bofors were to provide research and development facilities for a Krupps design team in return for the foreign rights on Krupp guns. From 1922 on, this research team was financed by the German War Office and Krupps set up a 'ghost' office under the name of Koch und Kienzle in Berlin as a cover for the Swedish team. From 1925 to 1930 the team worked on a 7.5 cm. L/60 anti-aircraft gun which could not reach War Office requirements, but some of these guns were manufactured for export to countries such as Spain and Brazil. When war broke out in 1939 undelivered 7.5 cm. guns were taken over by the

The Ehrhardt 5cm BAK (Ballon Abwehr Kanone), 1906.

7.7cm BAK by Daimler/ Krupp, 1910–1912.

German Navy and used for coastal defence.

In 1930–31, with the lessons of the unsuccessful 7.5 cm. gun behind them, the 'Swedish' team drew up detailed plans for an 8.8 cm. high velocity anti-aircraft gun. The choice of 8.8 cm. appears to have been dictated by the clause in the Versailles Treaty which stated that the Army could be equipped with 7.5 cm. and 10.5 cm. guns only. For anti-aircraft use the 7.5 cm. round had proved insufficiently powerful and a 10.5 cm. round was deemed too heavy for hand loading. Thus the designers plumped for the intermediate 8.8 cm. calibre. All details for the new gun were carefully checked out and in 1931 the plans were 'taken home' to Essen where a prototype was built by the end of the year.

Production plans were quietly made so that when the NSDAP came to power in 1933, the newly expanded Wehrmacht was able to take delivery of the new gun, the 8.8 cm. Flak 18 L/56.

The Flak 18 was an immediate success. It was a semi-automatic weapon in that when the gun fired it ejected its spent cartridge and recocked itself ready for use when the next round was loaded, either by hand or with the power-assisted rammer. The highly mobile carriage originally used two simple wheeled axles from which the gun was lowered for action. In action the gun could traverse through 360° on a cruciform platform with fold-up side arms which was originally designed for use with the unsuccessful 7.5 cm. gun. Range was sufficient to tackle any contemporary aircraft then contemplated for service.

Good as the gun was, the Heereswaffenamt (H.W.A., roughly equivalent to the Ministry of Supply) saw the need for some changes to the barrel assembly methods. This story of the 8.8 cm. gun barrel development is worthy of some study as it shows the detail in which the Germans were prepared to indulge in their preparations for war.

8.8 cm L/45 (Krupp).

(Below) 8.8 cm L/45 (Rheinmetall) in action

7.7 cm Kanone Flak by Daimler/Krupp, 1914.

5

Barrel Development.

The 8.8 cm. Flak 18 employed a conventional one-piece barrel which, with the cordite propellent and H.E. shells using the copper driving bands in use in 1933, had a life of about 900 rounds. This life was considered too short for the German War planners who anticipated a European war of short duration but great intensity. In the war conditions they envisaged, large numbers of worn barrels would need to be replaced imposing a strain on extended transport and repair facilities. Stockpiling of complete barrels would be prohibitively expensive and difficult due to the relative shortage of the high alloy steels needed. This problem was solved by the design team of Rheinmetall who came up with a three-piece barrel.

Their solution was based on the fact that most gun barrel wear takes place at the forcing cone and the first few calibres of rifling. The new barrel, known as the Rohr Aufbau 9 (R.A.9 – barrel construction 9) consisted of a jacket, a sleeve and an inner tube in three sections, the centre section of which carried the first part of the rifling and the forcing cone. A locking collar screwed the breech assembly to the jacket, and the three part inner tube was held in the sleeve by a clamping collar at the front of the barrel and a clamping ring at the rear. To change the inner sections the barrel could be stripped down in situ and the worn centre section only, replaced.

Four views of the 7.5cm L/60 anti-aircraft gun.

8.8cm L/45 (Krupp) ready for the road.

Thus instead of stockpiling complete barrels, only centre sections needed to be stored ready for use near the guns.

There were disadvantages to the new barrel. One was that high quality steel had to be used for its construction as the separate parts lacked the rigidity of a one-piece barrel. Manufacture had to be to very fine tolerances especially on the inner sections, and the number of man hours needed was well in excess of conventional construction. Also the weight of the finished product was greater than that of a normal barrel so carriage components such as the recoil and equilibriator mechanism had to be slightly modified.

All these disadvantages were recognised and

View from left

Loading tray

Cradle

Terminal box

Counter recoil mechanism
(Compressed air)

Cradle

Spring equilibrator

Traversing mechanism

Fuse setter attachment bracket

Pedestal

Levelling mechanism
(Gun platform)

Barrel support

Upper carriage cradle

Elevating mechanism
(Elevating gear)

Fuse setter

Levelling jack

Stake

8.8 cm Flak 18

View from right

Continuous-pointing traversing
wheel (Bearing)

Bearing receiver

Counter recoil mechanism
(Compressed air)

Spring equilibrator

Sighting mechanism

Traversing mechanism

Dial sight

Receiver (Altitude)

Barrel support

Breech actuating mechanism

Rammer guard

Loading tray

Auxiliary trigger

Sighting mechanism

Continuous-pointing traversing
wheel (Altitude)

Elevating mechanism
(Elevating gear)

Azimuth setter seat

8.8cm Flak 18

P.7002g

accepted for the R.A.9 conferred all the advantages needed of it. In large scale practice however, the system had to be modified to a two section inner barrel. This change was necessary as the joint between the chamber and the forcing cone centre section was wearing too quickly mainly due to gas leakage and grit introduced on the shells. Also the joint, covered by the front of the cartridge case, was subjected to slight temperature expansion differences leading to hard extraction and jams. To overcome this the chamber and centre sections were made in one piece.

The new R.A.9 barrel was introduced into service on the 8.8 cm. Flak 36, and the multi-section principle retained for the early production models of the 8.8 cm. Flak 41. But as the war continued the advantages of the sectioned barrel disappeared. One of the main reasons for this was that the introduction of new propellents such as diglycol and later Gudol, along with the replacement of copper driving bands by sintered iron, increased barrel life to as much as 10,000 rounds. So the original reason for the sectioned barrel disappeared and over-extended German industrial plants were left to mass-produce a barrel using high quality steel and an excessive number of man hours at a time when they could least afford it. Production lines could not be easily reorganised for simpler methods, and it was not until the last year of the war that it became possible to return to a simplified divided monobloc barrel for the Flak 18–37 series and the Flak 41. The choice of a divided monobloc was enforced rather than chosen as nearly all machinery in the factories had been designed to produce multi-section barrels and was therefore not large enough to produce one-piece barrels. At the end of the war some 8.8 cm. monobloc barrels were being made at the Skoda works, Pilsen, by using a new vertical centrifuge casting process.

In retrospect it can be seen that the introduction of the R.A.9 barrel was a typical example of German War planning that went badly wrong due to World War II lasting much longer than expected.

Close-up of the data transmission system of the 7.5cm L/60 FlAK (Flieger Abwehr Kanone).

Construction of the RA9 barrel.

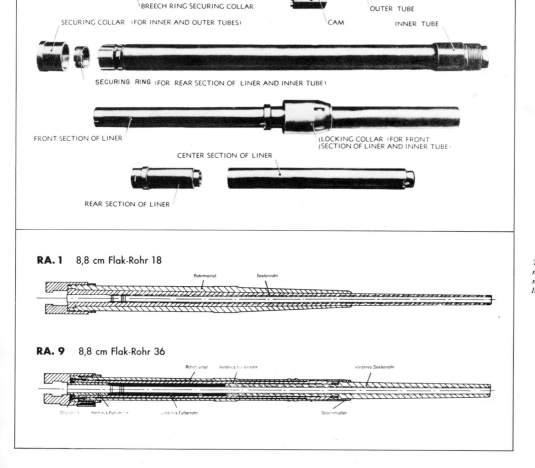

BREECH RING SECURING COLLAR

SECURING COLLAR (FOR INNER AND OUTER TUBES)

CAM

OUTER TUBE

INNER TUBE

SECURING RING (FOR REAR SECTION OF LINER AND INNER TUBE)

FRONT SECTION OF LINER

LOCKING COLLAR (FOR FRONT SECTION OF LINER AND INNER TUBE)

CENTER SECTION OF LINER

REAR SECTION OF LINER

RA. 1   8,8 cm Flak-Rohr 18

Rohrmantel   Seelenrohr

RA. 9   8,8 cm Flak-Rohr 36

Rohrmantel   hinteres Seelenrohr   vorderes Seelenrohr

hinteres Futterrohr   vorderes Futterrohr   Spannmutter

These cross-sections show the main differences between the monobloc and three-piece liner barrels.

Introduction of the Flak 36 and 37

As described in the last section the conversion of the 8.8 cm. Flak 18 to take the R.A.9 barrel resulted in a new designation, the 8.8 cm. Flak 36, L/56. Also introduced on the new gun was a new limber system, the Sonderhanger 201, designed by the firm of Linders. This new limber was designed after early experience with the 8.8 cm. Flak 18 in Spain where German 'Volunteers' had been assisting the Nationalist forces since 1936. The battle experience gained by the German units in Spain was to prove invaluable in the years to come, and as far as the '88' was concerned it led to the growing use of the gun as an indirect-fire artillery piece and eventually to the direct fire anti-tank role. In action it was found necessary to speed-up the time taken to get the gun into action and this led to the introduction of the Sonderhanger 201 mentioned above and eventually to the Sonderhanger 202 from 1939 onwards. This last carriage permitted the Flak 36 to be fired when still on its wheels, and the Sonderhanger 202 was retrofitted to the Flak 18. Most parts of the Flak 18 and 36 were directly interchangeable including barrels, which could also be interchanged with the Flak 37. The 8.8 cm. Flak 37 however, was intended purely for an anti-aircraft role and used a different fire control transmission system. The Flak 18 and 36 both used the Ubertragungsgerät 30 (U.T.G.30) which used a system involving lamps and pointers, but the Flak 37 used the later U.T.G.37 which was a selsyn, or 'follow the pointer' system. The Flak

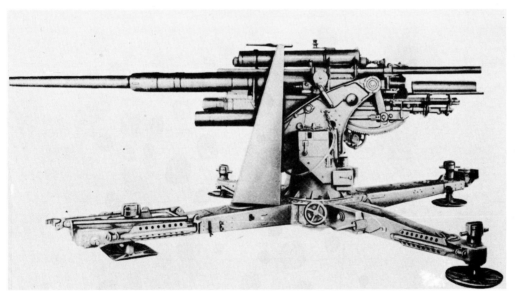

REAR BOGIE   FRONT BOGIE

Three views of the 8.8cm
Flak 36.

Another view of the 8.8cm Flak
18. (opposite above).

The nearest of these two 88s
has a one-piece Flak 18 type
barrel, while the other has a
barrel locking collar of the
RA9 construction – showing it
to be a Flak 36 or 37. (opposite
below).

37 also lacked the indirect and direct fire sighting systems introduced to the earlier models.

From 1938 onwards many Flak 18 and 36 guns were fitted with shields for crew protection and as a result of Spanish War experience, armour piercing ammunition was developed and issued from 1938 on.

Fuller details of the Flak 18, 36 and 37 can be found later in the book. The Flak 36 entered service in 1937 and the Flak 37 in 1939. Both types continued in production throughout the war, despite the introduction of more effective guns. A breakdown of the numbers of 8.8 cm. anti-aircraft guns is given here, but it must be stressed that there is no differentiation made between the different types and the figure includes the later Flak 41.

1940	1941	1942	1943	1944
1130	1872	2876	4416	5933

New Demands – the KwK 36 and Flak 41

While watching a demonstration of the Flak 36 during 1938, Hitler seems to have had one of his bouts of 'intuition' for he suggested to General Becker, then Director of Army Ordnance that the 8.8 cm. gun should be mounted horizontally for anti-tank use and also for mounting on tanks. The result of this was the 8.8 cm. KwK (Kampfwagenkanone) 36, L/56, mounted on the Tiger tank. For this role the gun was extensively modified, turned on its side, and a muzzle brake was fitted. For sheer power, the Tiger's armament put it streets ahead of all Allied tanks at the time of its introduction but the Tiger's massive size severely hampered its tactical mobility.

Another change to the story of the 8.8 cm. guns came in about 1937–38. By that time it became obvious to the German planners that aircraft development was increasing at such a rate that soon bomber aircraft would be able to fly at speeds and heights at which the 8.8 cm. Flak 18,

After the battle – an abandoned 8.8cm Flak 36 in Italy. (IWM).

This 8.8cm hybrid has Flak 37 fire control gear but a Flak 18 barrel, and is thus designated 8.8cm Flak 37. (IWM).

36 and 37 would be largely ineffective. Their immediate solution was to introduce larger calibre guns but a more powerful 8.8 cm. round was also envisaged. A new gun design for the new ammunition was called for and Rheinmetall were given the task.

Their new design was originally called the Gerät 37 but this was later changed to Gerät 41 and later the 8.8 cm. Flak 41 to prevent confusion with the existing 8.8 cm. Flak 37. A much more massive piece than the earlier guns it was also more complex and expensive. It did, however, meet its specification and continued in production for the rest of the war. By the time it was on the drawing board, the earlier Flak 18 and 36 had proved their value as dual-purpose weapons so the Flak 41 was intended from the start for possible anti-tank use. As a result it had a much lower silhouette than the earlier guns mainly brought about by the use of a turntable instead of a pedestal mounting. It suffered from one main fault and that was the constant problem of hard extraction and breech jams. This was brought about by the use of a multi-section barrel which was originally in five sections. Experience brought the number of sections down to three but the expansion of the sections in the long L/74 barrel led to tolerance build-ups at the

8.8cm Flak 37.

8.8cm Flak 37.

Close-up of the 8.8cm Flak 41 prototype.

breech which affected the steel cartridge cases. Brass cases gave no trouble but German resources could not provide enough brass in the quantities required, so steel cases and the resultant jams had to be tolerated.

One oddity of the Flak 41's career was that it was nearly rejected for service, not by the user arm but by Speer, the Minister for War Production, on the grounds it was too complex and expensive in manufacturing facilities. In March 1942 he was over-ruled by Hitler and a trial series of 44 guns built. These were sent off to North Africa, but only about half ever got there, the rest being sunk en route. When in Tunisia, the guns exhibited so many teething troubles that they spent more time in workshops than in the field, and all were left behind when the Germans left Africa. Hardly an auspicious start to a new weapon's career!

In attempts to increase the numbers of Flak 41 barrels in use, attempts were made to mount Flak 41 barrels on Flak 36 and 37 carriages but the excessive weight made this an awkward failure. Only in the last year of the war when simplified manufacturing methods led to a lighter Flak 41 barrel could this course be adopted, but by then it was too late.

Some Flak 41 barrels were mounted on the carriage of the 10.5 cm. Flak 39, and the new combination designated 8.8 cm. Flak 39/41. Only a few were made.

The 8.8cm KwK (Kampf-wagen Kanone)36 mounted on a Tiger 1.

Two views of the 8.8cm Flak 41 prototype at Meppen. ▶

The Battle against the Tank – The Pak 43

For some reason, Krupps were not asked to design a gun in competition with the 8.8 cm. Flak 41 until the early spring of 1941. Their design was designated the Gerät 42 and was intended to be the basis of a family of guns for all purposes. As well as the Flak piece it was intended to produce the KwK 42 and the Pak (Panzerabwehr-kanone) 42, all using the same ammunition. The Rheinmetall Flak 41 teething troubles ensured the continuing development of the Gerät 42 but early in 1943, improved anti-aircraft specifications were put forward by the Air Ministry. Krupps answered by dropping the Gerät 42 as the new demands could not be met without extensive re-design and development work and after February 1943, work was directed towards converting the Pak 42 and KwK 42 into the Pak 43 and KwK 43.

The 8.8 cm. Pak 43 L/71 was designed from the outset as an anti-tank gun only. As such it was probably the most effective and powerful piece used for the purpose to see service during World War II. An extremely well designed weapon, it had a low silhouette and was thus easy to conceal and difficult to hit. Protection for the crew came from a well-sloped armoured shield, and the piece was mounted on a mobile cruciform carriage which, when lowered from its limbers, gave a 360° traverse. The gun could also be fired direct from its wheeled carriage but when this occurred traverse was limited. In order to save materials and weight the barrel construction was relatively light and when using armour piercing ammunition only, barrel life was limited to 500 rounds.

At first, barrel production soon outstripped carriage production, and as demand from the Front grew in volume for the Pak 43, a makeshift expedient to give the troops an effective anti-tank gun produced the 8.8 cm Pak 43/41 L/71. This was the mounting of a Pak 43 barrel on the carriage of the 10.5 cm. le FH 18, using the wheels of the 15 cm. s.FH 18. The result looked high and clumsy but it worked and gave the hard pressed front line troops some protection against the Allied tank flood.

The Pak 43 was mounted on a variety of self-propelled carriages which are fully described in the appropriate section.

Designed for use in tanks, the 8.8 cm. KwK 43 was mounted in the Tiger II. It was closely allied to the Pak 43 and used the same ammunition. The combination of the KwK 43 and the Tiger II made up to what many believe was the most powerful tank of World War II.

Variants and Hybrids

As is only to be expected there were many minor variations on the 8.8 cm. theme. For instance there were many attempts to produce a better performance from the Flak 18–37 guns. One attempt that went further than most was the 8.8 cm. Flak 37/41, L/74. This was the use of a lengthened barrel with a muzzle brake to take Flak 41 ammunition. Only a few were built.

In order to increase the number of anti-aircraft guns for home defence of the Reich some captured Russian guns were re-bored to take 8.8 cm. ammunition. These were the 8.5/8.8 cm. Flak M.39 (r), the 7.62/8.8 cm. Flak M.38, and the 7.62/8.8 cm. Flak M.31 (r).

Many experimental guns were built to test theories on tapering bores, smooth bores, arrow shells, conical rifling, experimental ammunition etc., and these are more fully dealt with in the section on experimental equipment.

Three views of the 8.8cm Pak 43.

Wooden mock-up of the 8.8cm PAK (Panzer Abwehr Kanone) 43.

After the war many 8.8 cm. guns were taken over by countries which had been occupied by the Germans. Many survive now only as museum exhibits or trophies but some countries, such as Norway and Albania, retained them in service until at least the late '60's. In 1973 some Flak 36s were still in use in Spain.

DETAIL DESCRIPTIONS

The Mainstays, the Flak 18, 36 and 37
The main visual difference between the Flak 18 and Flak 36 was the barrel locking collar about one third of the way down from the muzzle. This collar was one of the locking devices for the multi-section (three or later two) barrel and was one of the parts removed to permit worn section replacement. Apart from the barrel the late Flak 18 and 36 were essentially similar, and early Flak 18 pieces were retrospectively modified up to Flak 36 standards. The work involved the modification of the early two-man laying system to one-man operation and the replacement of the early Linder-designed Sonderhanger 201 limber to the Sonderhanger 202 – again a Linder design. Visually, the main difference between the two is that the later limber had double pneumatic tyres on both 'halves' and that when being towed, the barrel pointed to the rear. Tactically, this had definite advantages when withdrawing from action over the earlier Sonderhanger 201 where the barrel pointed forwards.

The gun itself followed normal German practice in that it had a massive horizontal sliding

*8.8cm Flak 18 and SdKfz 7.
The gun is on a Sonderhänger
201 limber, with the barrel
pointing to the front as opposed
to the Sonderhänger 202 on
which it pointed to the rear.*

*8.8cm Flak 18 on pre-World
War II exercise in the Ruhr.*

*Hand-hauling a Flak 18 over
a pontoon bridge during the
1940 French campaign.*

*8·8cm Flak 18 on tow
behind an SdKfz 7. The gun is
mounted on a Sonderhanger
202.*

breech block, opening to the right. Breech actuation could be either manual or automatic. Ejection was automatic, and the one piece round could be loaded either by hand or with the assistance of a power-operated rammer from a 'fold over' loading tray. Firing was by a percussion mechanism cocked either by hand or automatically and employed the usual safeties. Triggering was by a lever to the left of the breech by the loading mechanisms.

The recoil mechanism of the 8.8 cm. Flak 18–37 was a hydropneumatic system with the recuperator cylinder above the barrel and the longer recoil cylinder beneath. Both cylinders used a glycerine-water mixture and nitrogen to absorb the firing forces and return the barrel to its firing position.

The gun was mounted on a cradle resting on two rearwards-curved trunnions which were, in turn, mounted on a pedestal. From this pedestal the gun could be levelled and traversed through 360°. The pedestal was fixed to the bottom carriage which consisted of a long box beam fore-and-aft, with upwards swinging outrigger arms which were swung down when in action. In action the gun could be fired from its limber with the outrigger arms lowered below the horizontal, but for prolonged use the carriage was lowered from the limbers and the side arms securely fixed in place with heavy bolts near the hinge. Also the outrigger arms were securely fixed in place with splined stakes hammered through the arms. Rough levelling of the arms was by levelling screw jacks at the arm extremities and fine levelling on the pedestal levelling mechanism.

When travelling the barrel was fixed rigidly by a hinged clamp on the main carriage member. In action the muzzle-heaviness of the gun was compensated for by two spring loaded equilibriators slung forward from the trunnions.

For fire control data transmission both the Flak 18 and 36 used the Ubertragungsgerät 30. Using this system the gun layer was presented with three concentric rings of small light bulbs. Data from the central predictor (a Kommandogerät 36 or 40) lit up one bulb on each ring which then had to be covered by one of three pointers. A 108-core cable was needed for this system and layers required extensive training to ensure smooth operation. The Flak 37 used the Ubertragungsgerät 37 system which employed a simpler selsyn or 'follow the pointer' method. This mechanism was able to fit into a radar con-controlled system and was also quicker and smoother to use. Briefly, electrical signals via a 46-core cable operated two pointers which were then followed mechanically by the layer.

When in use as an indirect fire field piece, the Flak 18 and 36 were laid using a Rundblickfernrohr 32 (Rbl.F.32) dial sight mounted on top of the recuperator cylinder over the barrel. The Flak 37 sometimes did not have this fixture. For sighting in a direct fire role, the layer used a Zielfernrohr 20 or 20E (ZF.20E) telescopic sight with range information coming from a hand-held rangefinder, the Entfernungsmessèr 34 (EM.34).

Fuze setting was effected on the Flak 18 and 36 by a fuze setting machine, the Zünderstellmaschine 18 (ZSM.18) mounted on the left trunnion side. It employed a light bulb and pointer mechanism similar to the fire control mechanism, while the ZSM.19 or 37 on the Flak

37 utilised a selsyn system. Both machines employed a similar fuze setting mechanism. When the nose of the shell was inserted into a cup one continuously rotating set of pawls engaged in a recess in the fuze, and turned the whole round until it came up against pre-set pawls. When this occurred the clockwork fuze mechanism was correctly set, the pawls disengaged, and the round was pushed out by a spring in the machine. Later in the war some Flak 37 guns were modified to take a ZSM.18/41 fuse setter which operated on the loading tray, thus reducing 'dead time'.

When used in an anti-tank role the A.P. round

Obviously a hit! A Flak 36 in action against tanks in Russia.

The end of a Flak 36 in the Western Desert. (IWM).

An 88 firing over open sights during street fighting in Italy.

8.8cm Flak 36 in action in Russia.

▼

could achieve the following penetrations against homogenous plate:—

Range in Yards	Normal Impact (90°)	Impact at 30°
500	5.07″	4.33″
1000	4.68″	3.97″
1500	4.33″	3.62″
2000	3.93″	3.30″

Details of the Flak 18, 36 and 37 follow:
8.8 cm. Flak 18, 36 and 37 data

Calibre	8.8 cm.	3.465″
Length of ordnance	4930 mm.	194″ (L/56)
Rifling	Right hand increasing	
Rifling length	4124 mm.	162 $\frac{7}{16}$″
No. of grooves	32	
Traverse	2 × 360°	
Elevation	−3° to +85°	
Recoil at 0°	1050 mm.	41.34″
Recoil at 25°	850 mm.	33.46″
Recoil at 85°	700 mm.	27.75″
Recoil maximum	1080 mm.	42.5″
Firing system	Percussion	
Rate of fire	15 – 20 rpm	
Ceiling – maximum	10,600 m.	34,770′
Ceiling – effective	8,000 m.	26,250′
Overall length	7620 mm.	25′
Overall height	2418 mm.	7′ 11″
Overall width	2305 mm.	7′ 7″
Weight complete	6861 kg.	15,129 lbs.
Time into action (6 men)	2½ mins.	
Time out of action (6 men)	3½ mins	
Muzzle velocity:		
HE time	820 m/s	2690 ft/sec.
HE percussion	820 m/s	2690 ft/sec.
APCBC	795 m/s	2600 ft/sec.

In August 1944 there were 10,930 Flak 18, 36 and 37 guns in service, compared with 2,600 guns in September 1939.

An 88 awaiting a target. Shells and trailer are ready for action in the side street.

A Flak 36 engaging Russian tanks during the last autumn of the war. The white rings on the barrel record the gun's successes: eleven tanks and six aircraft.

The KwK 36 L/56

Although the KwK 36 was developed from the Flak 36, and ballistically the two were identical, it differed in many respects from its originator. For a start the barrel was a one-piece design contained in a thin jacket. The breech block was vertical and firing was electrical, via a trigger on the elevating handwheel. A double baffle muzzle brake was fitted, but this was often unscrewed in transit, and carried internally.

The only vehicle to mount the KwK 36 was the Henschel SdKfz 181 Kpfw Tiger Model E (or Tiger I). In this massive tank, weighing 56 tons in action, the KwK 36 was mounted in the turret with full 360° traverse and −4° to +11° elevation. Traverse could be either by hand or by power controls actuated by the gunner's right foot. Because of the great turret weight the controls had to be low geared and therefore slow (it took 720 turns of the traverse handwheel to turn 360°). Elevation was by handwheel by the right of the gunner. The weight of the barrel was compensated for by a cylinder containing a large coil spring mounted on the left-hand front of the turret.

Direct sighting was a TZF 9b binocular tele-

Interior of a Tiger 1 tank turret showing the massive breech block of the KwK 36.

scope with an auxiliary clinometer for use in indirect laying. Also provided was a turret position indicator dial and the commander could use a SF 14Z stereoscopic telescope mounted on the cupola and an EM 34 coincidence rangefinder mounted on the turret roof. The commander also had a sighting vane mounted in his front episcope in the cupola for fire control in action.

The Tiger could carry 92 rounds stowed around and under the turret cage. This was more than enough for most tank engagements, and the Tiger/KwK 36 combination made this AFV the most powerful of its day. However, the great weight of the Tiger severely hampered its tactical mobility and the slow traverse of the turret was a great disadvantage in close combat. German documents dated March 1945 refer to the KwK 36 as 'obsolete'.

KwK 36 data

Length (calibres)	56.1
Length of piece	194.3″
Length of rifling	161.1″
Length of chamber	23.6″
Length of bore	184.7″
Length of bore (calibres)	53.3″
Length of muzzle brake	15.1″
Overall length of piece	209.4″
Weight of piece (complete)	2932 lbs.
Depth of breech opening	9.6″
Rifling − number of grooves	32
Depth of grooves	1.05 mm.
Width of grooves	5.34 mm.
Rifling twist	Increasing R.H. 1 in 45 to 1 in 30
Chamber capacity	3650 ccs.
Muzzle velocity	Pzgr. 38 (APC) 2,657 ft/sec.
	Pzgr. 40 (HVAP) 3,000 ft/sec.
	Gr. 39 HI (HEAT) 1,968 ft/sec.
	Sprgr. (HE) 2,690 ft/sec.

The Rheinmetall gun − the 8.8 cm. Flak 41, L/74

During the late '30's the development of the bomber aircraft was advancing rapidly and by 1938/39 the German war planners became painfully aware that the Flak 18–37 series was soon going to be unable to take on the high speed, high altitude raider. In 1939 Rheinmetall was given a contract for a new gun with sufficient muzzle velocity to reach higher altitudes. This was thought feasible due to the new Gudol propellent along with the development of sintered iron driving bands. Designated Gerät 37 the new gun had to be capable of anti-tank use. Power controls were not to be employed in order to keep down weight. Briefly, the specification contained the following:—

Muzzle velocity	1000 m/s. (3280 ft/sec.) at least
Shell weight	9.4 kg. (20.7 lbs)
Weight in action	8000 kg. (approx. 8 tons) maximum
Rate of fire	25 rounds/min.

To prevent confusion with the Flak 37 the designation was changed in the summer of 1941 to 8.8 cm. Flak 41, at the same time as the gun was ready for initial trials. During these trials brass cartridge cases were used which disguised the later hard extraction troubles with steel cases, but there were many other teething troubles. The gun, like most Rheinmetall designs, bristled with new and untried features among which was a multi-section barrel made up of five parts. But by the winter of 1941 it became apparent that despite the troubles still not ironed out there was no alternative to the Flak 41 in sight so the gun was ordered into production in the Spring of 1942. It was not until early 1943 that the first guns reached the troops, and, as has already been related, these were sent to North Africa.

Designed from the outset as a dual-purpose weapon, the Flak 41 was a great improvement on the earlier guns. It was, however, complex, massive and expensive. These latter factors led to the Reichsminister Speer insisting on its cancellation but he was over-ruled by Hitler himself and the project went ahead. An example of the complexity was that the gun employed no fewer than three separate electrical firing mechanisms. They were:—
1) For anti-aircraft fire.
2) For direct fire against ground or sea targets.
3) An emergency firing mechanism.

The mounting was on a turntable which considerably lowered the gun's silhouette and the piece continued to use the Sonderhanger 202. Guns produced for purely static use employed the later Sonderhanger 203 when in transit. A

Two views of the 8.8cm Flak 41.

$\frac{5}{16}''$ thick shield was fitted for crew protection.

The considerably lengthened barrel (L/74) and lack of power controls made elevation by the single layer so difficult that an extra man had to assist in this task. Data transmission to the gun continued to be via the U.T.G.37 but the fuze setter was the newer ZSM.41 which operated on two horizontal loading trays hinged to the side of the carriage. Each tray had a setting head and the round was rotated on rollers as the fuze setting mechanism operated. From the loading tray, the round was loaded by a 'power operated' mechanism with the 'power' coming from an auxiliary hydro-pneumatic recuperator gear. When released, the mechanism pushed the round into rotating rubber rollers which impelled it into the chamber.

Use of the multi-section barrel gave rise to considerable expansion differentials due to temperature differences in the barrel. With the steel cartridge cases in use this led to continual breech jams caused by hard extraction which were the

Flak 41's biggest bugbear. With this in mind, and also to reduce barrel wear, crews were instructed to leave the gun to cool for five minutes after every 20–25 rounds fired, but this ruling had to be ignored in action. In an attempt to reduce these troubles the number of barrel sections was reduced to four and finally three parts. A breakdown of this follows.

Late production Tiger Ausf.E or Tiger 1, the only vehicle to mount the KwK 36. (Bundesarchiv).

Barrel Nos. 0001–0152	Five sections
Jacket	
Sleeve	
Forward section inner tube	
Central section inner tube	
Chamber section inner tube	
Barrel Nos. 0153–0285	Four sections
Jacket	
Sleeve	
Forward section inner tube	
Rear section inner tube	
Barrel No. 0286 on.	Three sections
Jacket	
Forward section inner tube	
Rear section inner tube	

Barrel Nos. 0001–0152 were cleared for use with brass cartridge cases only. Life for four and three section barrels was usually about 1500 rounds. Despite its troubles the Flak 41 was an outstanding anti-aircraft gun to the extent that it could out-perform the heavier 10.5 cm. Flak 38 and 39. As far as the defence of the Reich was concerned there were never enough of them. In February 1945 there were 279 in use in Germany and they were carefully emplaced, sometimes on Flak towers, around targets of prime importance.

There were many attempts to use the Flak 41 barrel on other equipments. One, the abortive 8.8 cm. Flak 39/41 has already been mentioned, but this, like all others, was not adopted for large scale service for the simple reason that there were not enough barrels being produced for the carriage designed for the Flak 41.

8.8 cm. Flak 41 Data

Length	74 calibres	
Length of ordnance	6548 mm.	257¾″
Rifling	Right hand increasing	
Rifling length	5411 mm.	213″
No. of grooves	32	
Traverse	360°	
Elevation	−3° to +90°	
Recoil at 0°	1200 mm.	47″
Recoil at 90°	900 mm.	35½″
Firing system	Electrical	
Rate of fire	15 r.p.m.	
Ceiling maximum	15000 m.	49200′
Overall length	9650 mm.	31′8″
Overall height	2360 mm.	7′9″
Overall width	2400 mm.	7′10½″
Weight complete	11240 kg.	24784 lbs.
Muzzle velocity:		
HE Time	1000m/s.	3280 ft/sec.
HE Percussion	1000m/s.	3280 ft/sec.
APCBC	980m/s.	3214 ft/sec.

Attempting to improve the breed — the 8.8 cm. Flak 37/41

By 1942, with the new Flak 41 just starting production it became obvious to the German Air Ministry that the Flak 18–37 series would have to bear the brunt of the German anti-aircraft defences for some considerable time to come and thought was given to modifying the earlier pieces to take the more powerful and larger Flak 41 round. Attempts to simply fit a Flak 41 barrel to a Flak 36 carriage did not work as the stresses produced were too great, and anyway there were simply not enough Flak 41 barrels being produced. Trials were also carried out using re-chambered Flak 37 barrels with muzzle brakes. The results of trials with L/56 and later L/66 barrels showed that Flak 41 performance could be achieved by increasing the barrel length to L/74 and fitting a muzzle brake made up of an extra length of barrel with two holes drilled each side next to two screwed-on flange plates. Both smooth bore and rifled brakes were tried and the efficiency was 45%. Extra strengthening was carried out on the equilibriators and the breech ring.

Barrel modifications on the one piece Flak 18 barrel were fairly straightforward but the multi-

Two views of the 8.8cm Flak 41.

section liners of the Flak 36 and 37 had to be replaced by a new one-piece barrel. The same power rammer and horizontal fuze setter as already produced for the Flak 41 were fitted and the U.T.G.37 data transmission system retained.

The Flak 37/41 met its design requirements but was not produced in any quantity. One source states that only 13 barrels had been produced by February 1945. A possible reason is that there was considerable trouble with the extraction of the steel-cased ammunition – a snag carried over from the Flak 41.

8.8 cm. Flak 37/41 Data

Length of ordnance	7027 m.	23′0⅝″
Length (calibres)	74	
Length (calibres) plus muzzle brake	80	
Length of chamber	881 mm.	2′10″
Length of rifling	5850 mm.	19′2½″
Length of unsupported barrel	3619 mm.	11′10½″
Length of breech ring	540 mm.	1′9¼″
Rifling	Right hand increasing	
Rifling grooves (No.)	32	
Rifling width	5.2 mm.	.2047″
Rifling depth	1.05 mm.	.0413″
Traverse	360°	
Elevation	−3° to +85°	
Firing system	Electrical or mechanical	
Rate of fire	16 – 20 r.p.m.	
Maximum ceiling	15000 m.	49,200′
Weight complete	7111 kg.	7 tons
Muzzle velocity HE	1000 m/s.	3280 ft/sec.
APCBC	980 m/s.	3214 ft/sec.

Undeveloped Potential – the Gerät 42

It was normal German practice when specifications were produced for a new anti-aircraft gun to give competing orders to both Krupp and Rheinmetall, but when the specification which led to the 8.8 cm. Flak 41 was issued only Rheinmetall was invited to tender. This odd deviation from normal procedure may be explained by the fact that Rheinmetall came under the cover of the Reichswerk Hermann Goering, so probably political strings were pulled in the Air Ministry and H.W.A. But by the spring of 1941 the Gerät 37, later to be the Flak 41 was already showing signs of future troubles and an 'insurance' order was issued to Krupps under the designation Gerät 42.

The specification called for a 10 kg. shell and a muzzle velocity of 1020 m./s. Krupps, with the thoroughness and attention to detail which showed in all their gun designs, intended the Gerät 42 to be part of a family of guns which included a Pak 42 and a KwK 42 all using the same ammunition. It was hoped that the construction of a prototype would be completed by the spring of 1943 but before that happened G.L. Flak issued a new specification, as follows:—

Shell weight	9.4 kg.	20.7 lbs.
Round weight	23 kg.	51.6 lbs.
Muzzle velocity	1100 m/s.	3610 ft/sec.
Round length	1220 mm.	48″
Barrel length	L/80	23′ 1″
Barrel weight	1920 kg.	38 cwt.

The new specification meant that the Gerät 42 (by then re-designated the Flak 42) would have had to be extensively revised, so in February 1943 the whole Flak 42 project was dropped and the design staffs were diverted to much needed tank and anti-tank gun projects.

Gerät 42 Data

Length of piece	L/75
Length of rifling	L/59
Muzzle velocity	1000 m/s.
Chamber capacity	90 litres
Muzzle brake efficiency	55%
Weight of piece	1840 kg.
Weight complete	7700 kg.
Height of trunnions	1350 mm.
Traverse	360°
Elevation	−3° to +90°
Rate of fire	22–25 r.p.m.
Shell weight	10 kg.
Charge weight	6.75 kg.
Type of propellent	Gudol
Length of round	1220 mm.
Weight of round	20 kg.

Tank killer – the 8.8 cm. Pak 43

With the passing of the Flak 42 the Krupp design staff was able to pass on to the design of a new anti-tank gun for the Wehrmacht. This new gun was urgently needed as the anti-tank guns in service with the front line troops were fast reaching the limits of their development and enemy AFV's, especially the later T-34 variants and the JS-I and II, were becoming increasingly invulnerable to frontal assault. Something heavier and more powerful was needed quckly, and Krupps came up, just in time, with the 8.8 cm. Pak 43, L/71, introduced in late 1943 and developed from the defunct Pak 42.

Whichever way it is approached, the Pak 43 was probably the finest and best designed anti-tank gun produced in World War II. Owing much to the earlier experiences gained with the Flak

Two views of the wooden model of the projected Gerät 42 auf Sonderfahrgestell.

18–37 series, it embodied a low, well protected barrel on a cruciform platform giving 360° traverse and similar to existing anti-aircraft carriages. In transit the gun (with double baffle muzzle brake) was mounted on two single axle bogies and could be fired from them although traverse was limited to 30° either side without the outrigger arms in place. Ideally, the piece was lowered from the bogies and dug in, when the height was lowered to only about 4′ 6″ with the swing out outrigger arms fixed firmly in place. The full 360° traverse was then possible.

Firing of the piece was by an electrical circuit. At high angles of elevation (above +28°) cutout switches prevented the recoiling breech hitting one of the cruciform members and the trigger was fitted to the elevating handwheel. The breech was unusual for a German design in being of the semi-automatic vertical falling block variety. Crew protection was afforded by a well sloped armoured shield.

Direct laying was via a Zielenrichtung 43 V So. with a $3 \times 8°$ or $3 \times 8°/11$ telescope. An Aushilfs-richtmittel 38 auxiliary sight was provided for indirect fire.

The high velocity fire produced by this remarkable piece could destroy any Allied vehicle. Also, the wide range of ammunition developed and available (described below) enabled the gun to be used to its full potential. But it is only fair to remark that with the Pak 43 the 8.8 cm. line had just about reached the peak of its conventional development potential. This can be seen by the fact that the barrel life, although it was rather lightly constructed to save weight and materials, was limited to about 500 rounds of the high velocity armour piercing ammunition.

The Pak 43 was mounted on a variety of self propelled mounting described in the appropriate section.

Close-up of breech of the 8.8cm Pak 43.

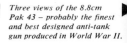

Three views of the 8.8cm Pak 43 – probably the finest and best designed anti-tank gun produced in World War II.

8.8 cm. Pak 43, L/71 Data

Length of ordnance	6610 mm.	260.23″
Rifling	Uniform right hand twist	
Rifling length	5125 mm.	201.75″
No. of grooves	32	
Chamber length	859 mm.	33.88″
Chamber capacity	9000 cc.	549 cu. ins.
Traverse	360°	
Elevation	−8° to +40°	
Recoil normal	750 mm.	29.5″
Recoil maximum	1200 mm.	47.25″
Overall length	9200 mm.	30′ 2″
Overall height	2050 mm.	6′ 9″
Overall width	2200 mm.	7′ 2½″
Weight complete	5000 kg	11,025 lbs.
Muzzle velocities:		
8.8 cm. Sprgr.Patr.KwK 43	700 m/s.	2298 ft/sec.
8.8 cm. Sprgr.Patr.43 KwK 43	750 m/s.	2460 ft/sec.
8.8 cm. Pzgr.Patr.39–1 KwK 43	1000 m/s.	3282 ft/sec.
8.8 cm. Pzgr.Patr.39/43 KwK 43	1000 m/s.	3282 ft/sec.
8.8 cm. Pzgr.Patr.40/43 KwK 43	1130 m/s.	3708 ft/sec.
8.8 cm. Gr.Patr.39 HL.KwK 43	600 m/s.	1968 ft/sec.
8.8 cm. Gr.Patr.39/43 HL.KwK 43	600 m/s.	1968 ft/sec.

Armour Penetration

Using 8.8 cm. Pzgr. Patr. 39/43

Range (yds)	Penetration 90° (mm)	Penetration 30° (mm)
0	225	198
500	207	182
1000	190	167
1500	174	153
2000	159	139
2500	145	127

Using 8.8 cm. Pzgr. Patr. 40/43

Range (yds)	Penetration 90° (mm)	Penetration 30° (mm)
0	311	265
500	274	226
1000	241	192
1500	211	162
2000	184	136
2500	159	114

American troops test firing a captured Pak 43. The gun was one of a number captured in a railway yard at Rheims and was later used against its former owners.

Mounting for an 8.8cm Pak 43/41.

The Stopgap — the 8.8 cm. Pak 43/41. L/71

When first introduced to the hard-pressed front-line troops, the Pak 43 was a great and immediate success. Not surprisingly, formation commanders on all fronts announced that they could not survive without the new weapon and demands flooded into the Krupp factories. It was at this juncture (early in 1944) that the RAF weighed in to severely disrupt carriage production and for a time gun production outstripped carriage output. Demand for the new gun was so heavy that an alternative carriage was desperately sought for. Captured Russian 15.2 cm. howitzer and French 155 mm. howitzer carriages were considered, tried and rejected as too heavy and awkward (both were used as makeshift carriages for the 12.8 cm. Pak 44 later in the war), and the eventual solution was a hodge-podge of existing German components. The main carriage chosen was that of the 10.5 cm. le F.H.18, just going out of production in favour of the 10.5 cm. le F.H.18/40 and the wheels of the 15 cm. s.F.H.18. Short split trails from the 10.5 cm. le F.H.18 were retained and a new shield provided. Ballistically the gun was the same as the Pak 43, but the breech mechanism was simplified and provision made for dial sights to enable the piece to be used as a field gun. The dial sight was an Rbl.32 or 36 mounted over the direct laying telescope.

In action, the Pak 43/41 looked, and was, high, clumsy and nose heavy. But it had the sole saving grace in that it worked and gave the front-line troops added protection against the ever-growing number of Allied tanks encountered on all fronts. Like the Pak 43, there was never enough of them, a fact that many Allied tank crews could be grateful for.

8.8 cm. Pak 43/41. L/71 Data

Length of ordnance	6616 mm.	260.23″
Rifling	Right hand twist	
Rifling length	5125 mm.	201.75″
No. of grooves	32	
Chamber length	859 mm.	33.88″
Chamber capacity	9000 cc.	549 cu. ins.
Traverse	56°	
Elevation	−5° to +38°	
Recoil normal	680 mm.	26.77″
Recoil maximum	720 mm.	28.35″
Overall length	9144 mm.	30′1″
Overall height	1981 mm.	5′8″
Overall width	2527 mm.	8′3½″
Weight complete	4380 kg.	9656 lbs.
Muzzle velocity	As Pak 43	
Armour penetration	As Pak 43	

Close-up of the 8.8cm Pak 43/41 breech and mounting.

Fig. 7

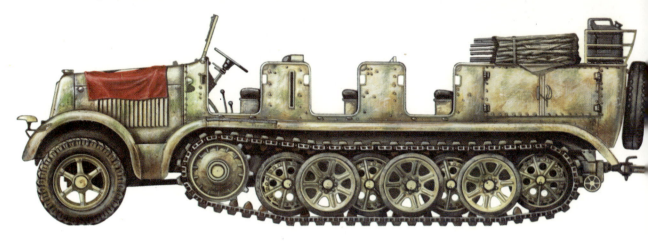

Middle left and bottom right: Side and top views of 8·8 cm Flak 18.

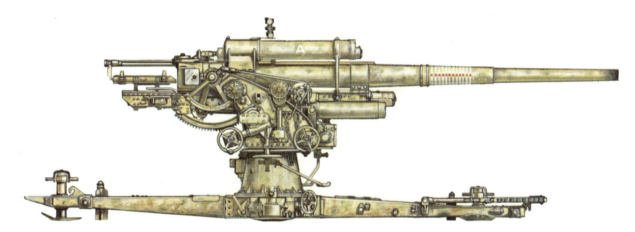

Bottom left: 8·8 cm Flak 41 auf Sonderfahrgestell.

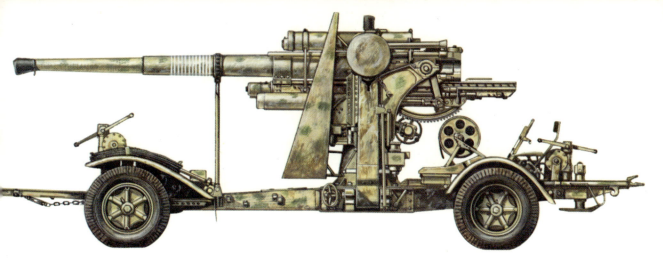

Top: 8·8 cm Flak 18 on a Sonderhänger 201 on tow behind an 8 ton Zugkraftwagen SdKfz 7.

Ammunition (*not to scale*)

1 8·8 cm. Panzergranate Patrone 39. APCBC.

2 8·8 cm. Panzergranate Patrone (mit Bd.Z.). HEAT.

3 8·8 cm. Sprenggranate Patrone L/4·5 (Kz.) (Ub.). Practice HE round.

4 8·8 cm. Sprenggranate Patrone L/4·5 (Kz.) (Bl.). Blank shell and cartridge.

5 8·8 cm. Sprenggranate Patrone L/4·5 (Kz.). HE shell with cast filling.

6 8·8 cm. Panzergranate Patrone (Üb.). Practice round—lead filled.

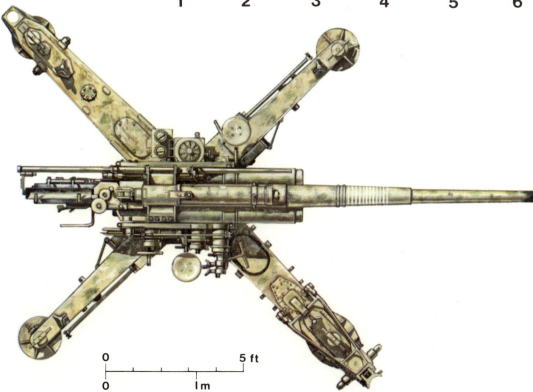

A Pak 43/41 on tow by a Schwerer Wehrmacht-sschlepper.

A Pak 43/41 in action against its former owners near Metz in early 1945. (IWM).

Ordnance for a King – the 8.8 cm. KwK 43. L/71

Developed from the proposed 8.8 cm. KwK 42 the 8.8 cm. KwK 43 was fitted to only one AFV, the SdKfz 182 Tiger II (Ausf.B) known to the Allies as the 'King or Royal Tiger' and to the Germans as the 'Koenigstiger'. Ballistically the KwK 43 was identical to the Pak 43 and differed only in having the two recoil cylinders mounted over the two-piece barrel and being slightly longer. At first, it was intended to fit 15 cm. or 10.5 cm. guns to the Tiger II, but Hitler intervened to insist on the installation of the KwK 43, the result being what many armour experts believe was the most powerful tank in service in World War II. The KwK 43 was also intended for installation in the Schmallturm of the Panther II.

The KwK 43 was mounted 3.1″ to the right of the turret centre line in the Tiger II's 360° traverse turret. Two types of turret, the Porsche and the Henschel, were produced with slightly differing mountings for the gun but the main production variant using the Henschel turret had a large Saukopf cast mantlet over the gun/turret mounting. Stowed in the rear turret bulge were 22 rounds – 11 a side – ready for use with a further 48 rounds stowed in panniers on each side of the hull. A further ten rounds were carried loose in various locations making a total of 80 rounds in all, usually split 40 HE/40 APCBC. The gunner was equipped with a standard TZF 9d or 9b1 monocular sight and had the option of power or manual traverse. To overcome the barrel weight when elevating a hydro-pneumatic cylinder was fitted between the recoil cylinders and mounting.

The Tiger II first saw service in May 1943 on the Russian Front and soon established itself as a formidable opponent. The vehicle's great weight (68 tons 13 cwt. with the Henschel turret) severely hampered its mobility, which, together with a short engine life and mechanical breakdowns, imposed a mainly defensive tactical role on the Tiger II, but it remained in service for the remainder of the war.

In early 1945 in an attempt to boost the performance of the KwK 43 still further, design work started on a proposal to lengthen the barrel from L/71 to L/105. This design never left the drawing board as a decision had been made to drop high velocity tank and anti-tank weapons in favour of cheaper low velocity smooth-bore guns firing finned missiles with hollow charge warheads. The end of the war intervened before development work had been completed on these new weapons.

8.8 cm. KwK 43 L/71

Length of piece	71.6 calibres	
Length of bore	6038.5 mm.	237.6″ (68.6 cals)
Length of chamber	859.5 mm.	33.8″
Chamber capacity	9000 cu. cm.	549 cu. ins.
Length of rifling	5179 mm.	203.8″
Rifling No. of grooves	32	
Rifling	Uniform right hand twist	1 in 27.57
Weight complete	3	3726 lbs.
Muzzle velocity	As Pak 43	

The Russian Guns

The start of 'Operation Barbarossa' against Russia in 1941 brought an immense amount of captured war material into the German armoury. Included in the vast haul were the three standard Russian heavy anti-aircraft guns, the 7.62 cm. Model 1931, the 7.62 cm. Model 1938, and the 8.5 cm. Model 1939. All three guns were competent, straightforward designs on mobile cruciform carriages similar to the 8.8 cm. carriage but generally less complex with two simple single-axle bogies. All three types of gun were appropriated for defence of the Reich and were issued to some second line Army units but also to Auxiliary Flak units made up from factory workers, Hitler Jugend and reservists. Captured Russian ammunition was used until supplies ran out, when the barrels were rebored to 8.8 cm. to take Flak 18–37 ammunition. The reboring operation was carried out in Northern Italy during 1943.

Only a few of the 96 Model 1931 guns were used, redesignated 7.62 cm. Flak M.31 (r) were

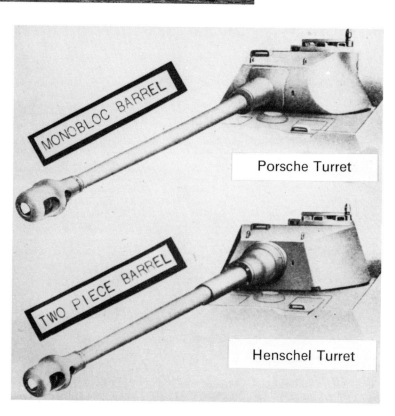

Porsche Turret

Henschel Turret

The 8.8cm Kwk 43 L/71 had a monobloc barrel in the Porsche turret of the Koenigstiger, the Tiger II, and a two-piece barrel in the Henschel turret.

rebored as the barrel was not up to the performances required of it and most were scrapped during 1944. The other two guns, the 7.62 Model 1938 and the 8.5 cm. Model 1939, redesignated 7.62 cm. Flak M.38 (r) and 8.5 cm. Flak M.39 (r) respectively were similar in all respects except the gun calibres and the muzzle brake on the Model 1939. When rebored they became the 7.62/8.8 cm. Flak M.38 (r) and 8.5/8.8 cm. Flak M.39 (r) and continued in service until the end of the war. One source states that 192 of the two more modern guns were used, but although only

a few 7.62/8.8 cm. Flak 31 (r) guns were produced exact numbers are not recorded.

Russian Gun Data

	7.62/8.8 cm. Flak M.31(r)	7.62/8.8 cm. Flak M.38(r)	8.5/8.8 cm. Flak M.39(r)
Length (calibres)	55	55	55.2
Weight complete (kg)	4820	4210	4220
Length overall (mm)	6700	5150	5150
Width emplaced (mm)	2210	4800	4800
Width mobile (mm)	1300	2250	2250
Height (mm)	2320	2220	2220
Weight emplaced (kg)	3650	3047	3057
Length of barrel (mm)	4191	4191	4693
Number of rifled grooves	32	32	32
Barrel weight (kg)	830	920	920
Traverse	360°	360°	360°
Elevation	−2° to +82°	−3° to +82°	+2° to +82°
Crew	11	11	11

8.8 cm. Naval Guns

Although of an entirely different family from the 8.8 cm. Flak guns, the German 8.8 cm. naval guns are included to 'complete the picture'. Used both as ship mounted dual-purpose weapons and coastal defence guns these four types are best summarised in brief tabular form.

	8.8 cm. SKC/30	8.8 cm. SKC/31	8.8 cm. SKC/32	8.8 cm. SKC/35
Beginning of development	1930	1931	1932	1935
Projectile weight (kg.)	9.0	9.0	9.0	9.0
Muzzle velocity (metres/sec.)	790	1060	950	700
Bore length (calibres)	42	72	72	42
Bore length (mm.)	3700	6330	6330	3700
Gun length (calibres)	45	75	75	45
Gun length (mm.)	3960	6600	6600	3960
Number of grooves	24	28	28	24
Chamber length (mm.)	530	843	530	?

Self Propelled Carriages

The earliest attempt to increase the tactical mobility of the 8.8 cm. series was the mounting of the 8.8 cm. Flak 18 on a 12-ton half track artillery tractor as the 8.8 cm. Flak 18 auf Selbstfahrlafette Zugkraftwagen 12t. Vehicles so converted took part in the 1940 French campaign but the project appears to have been discontinued. Weight was about 17 tons.

The next attempt to use a half-track mounting involved the Flak 37 on the 18-ton half-track. This was the 8.8 cm. Flak 37 (SF) auf Zugkraftwagen 18t (SdKfz 9/1), and 14 of these large

8.8cm KwK 43 with two-piece barrel mounted in the Henschel turret of a Koenigstiger. (Bundesarchiv.)

tractors were converted at Weserhuette, Bad Oeynhausen. On this mounting the gun had a full 360° traverse once the mesh sides had been lowered for a working platform and four small outrigger arms swung down. There was no protection for the nine-man gun crew but the engine and driver's compartment were covered by 14.5 mm. armour. In use these 25 ton vehicles were intended for anti-aircraft protection of mobile columns though some sources state that

they also had an anti-tank role. This latter role seems unlikely in view of the Flak 37's unsuitability for the task.

Another Flak 37 self-propelled mounting, dating from autumn 1940, was an experimental fully tracked chassis designed by Krupp and using Panzer IV and half-track components. This was the 8.8 cm. Flak 37 auf Sonderfahrgestell. Weighing 20 tons the vehicle's hull top was a flat platform for the Flak 37 with a full

76.2/8.8cm Flak M31(r).

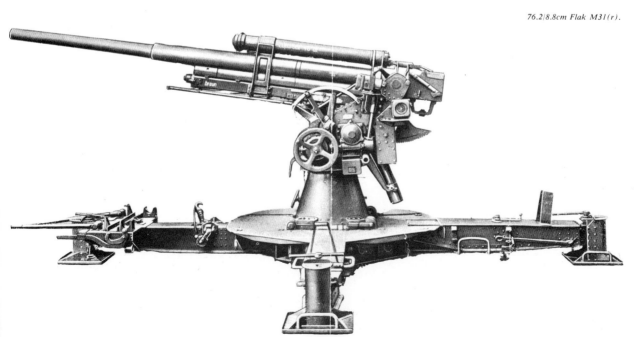

76.2/8.8cm Flak M39(r).

Three views of the Flak 37 auf Sonderfahrgestell. (below and opposite).

360° traverse. Crew protection in transit came from the gun shield and fold-up armour at the sides and rear. In action though, the sides were lowered to act as a working platform for the eight man crew, who were thus left unprotected. Only one of these vehicles, sometimes referred to as Flakpanzer fuer Schwere Flak, or Grille 10, was built and later, in 1944, the Flak 37 was replaced by an 8.8 cm. Flak 41 for extensive field trials. Weight was increased to 23 tons but the combination was not developed for service use. Outside dimensions of the vehicle were 7000 × 3000 ×2800 mm.

One vehicle that did not leave the wooden mock-up stage was designated '8.8 cm. Kanone

8.8cm Flak 18 auf Selbst-fahrlafette Zugkraftwagen 12t.

Flak 37 auf Sonderfahrgestell.

8.8cm Flak 37 (Sf) auf Zugkraftwagen 18t.

8.8cm Flak 37 (Sf) auf Zugkraftwagen 18t ready for the road.

(Pz.Sf1) auf Sonderfahrgestell' or '8.8 cm. Kanone fuer gepanzererte Selbstfahrlafette IVc'. Intended originally as a self propelled mounting for an 8.8 cm. variant that finally emerged as the 8.8 cm. KwK 36, it was later intended to mount the 8.8 cm. Pak 43. Three prototypes were ordered from Krupps in the autumn of 1941 to be completed by the autumn of 1943, but the vehicles were never built, probably because of the difficulties in producing an entirely new vehicle when existing equipments were needed in large quantities. Weight of the new vehicle was originally specified as 22 metric tons but this later rose to 30 tons. Armour varied from 10–50 mm. and was later intended to be up to 80 mm. thick. Power source was a Maybach 'HL90' 12-cylinder 'V' 9.99-litre petrol engine delivering 400 b.h.p. at 4000 r.p.m. Performance anticipated was about 35 km./hr. Crew strength would have been five.

Soon after its introduction into service in 1943 the 8.8 cm. Pak 43 went 'mobile' in some numbers and on a variety of chassis. In order to suit the wide variety of mountings encountered the specialised mountings were identified by the addition of a sub-type. Listed below are the vehicles involved:—

Sd Kfz 164/1	8.8 cm. Pak 43/1 L/71 auf Panzerjäger III/IV (Nashorn)
Sd Kfz 184	8.8 cm. Pak 43/2 L/71 auf Panzerjäger Tiger P (Elefant)
Sd Kfz 173	8.8 cm. Pak 43/3 L/71 auf Panzerjäger Panther (Jagdpanther)
	8.8 cm. Pak 43/3 auf Selbstfahrlafette 38(d)
	8.8 cm. Pak 43/3 auf Panzerjäger 38(t)
	8.8 cm. Pak 43/3 auf Krupp/Steyr Selbstfahrlafette 38(d)
Sd Kfz 186	8.8 cm. Pak 43/3 auf Panzerjäger Tiger ausf B (Jagdtiger)

Starting from the top of this list, the Nashorn can be regarded as a stop-gap Panzerjäger or tank-killer until more specialised vehicles became available. Built on a chassis with a Panzer III drive and track made up from Panzer IV components the Pak 43/1 mounting was behind a thinly armoured and open-topped fighting compartment on the rear of the vehicle. Rather high and heavy for its task the Nashorn (or Hornisse) saw extensive service since 473 were built by the Deutsche-Eisenwerke at Teplitz-Schoenau. In action, it carried 40 rounds and a crew of five. Weight was 26.5 tons.

The 8.8 cm. Pak 43/2 was mounted on the Elefant (or Ferdinand) chassis, which was probably the biggest failure of the entire German armament industry. The Elefant chassis started life as the hull for the VK 4501 Tiger (P) tank prototypes. This Porsche design never saw production as a tank since the production contract it was built for went to Henschel who produced the Tiger I. In order not to waste the effort put into the Tiger (P) project the chassis and hulls were converted to self-propelled mounts for the 8.8 cm. Pak 43/2 for use as Panzerjäger. (For some reason the 8.8 cm. gun mounted on the Elefant was initially known as the 8.8 cm. Stu.K. 43/1 (L71) (Sturmkanone 43/1) but in all respects it was identical to the mobile 8.8 cm. Pak 43 so the designation was later changed to Pak 43/2). The production run went to 90 vehicles, mainly built by Niebelungwerke at St. Valentin, and later also by Alkett of Berlin-Spandau. All 90 vehicles were used in the disastrous Kursk offensive on the Russian Front in July 1943 where they were decimated by infantry tank killer squads for the simple reason they carried no auxiliary armament for close-in defence. Some of the survivors later saw limited service in Italy. Overweight (68 tons) and mechanically unreliable (the electrical-mechanical drive was insufficiently developed and gave constant trouble) the Elefant passed from the scene with few regrets from the Panzerjäger units. In action carried 50 rounds and a crew of six.

In contrast, the Jagdpanther was a great success as a tank-killer. Built on to a Panzer V Panther chassis, the 8.8 cm. Pak 43/3 fighting compartment was well protected behind sloping armour and the vehicle was fast and highly mobile. Production by M.I.A.G. started in December 1943 and 382 were built. Rightly regarded by the Allies as a formidable opponent, the Jagdpanther saw extensive service on all fronts. It weighed 45.5 tons, carried a crew of

8.8cm Pak 43/1 L/71 on the Pzkw III/IV – the Nashorn or Hornisse. (Bundesarchiv).

five and 60 rounds.

The next three vehicles in the above list were all 1944/45 prototype vehicles based on the German developed version of the Czech 38(t) tank chassis. They all carried the 8.8 cm. Pak 43/3 in open 360° traverse turrets, and were intended not so much as Panzerjäger but as prototype Waffentrager weapon carriers. None of them was thought suitable for service, although some were used in action in 1945, and further design work was planned by Ardelt in conjunction with Krupps. All three vehicles

mentioned weighed between 15 and 15.5 tons. Projected designs incorporated 360° traverse mountings, for a variety of weapons (including the 8.8 cm. KwK 43), and more limited armour protection.

The 8.8 cm. Pak 43/3 gun was mounted on only a few of the 70-ton Jagdtiger monsters. They were fitted only when RAF bomber raids disrupted production of the vehicle's normal armament, the 12.8 cm. Pak 44 or 80, L/55.

One odd use of the 8.8 cm. KwK 43 tank gun was the mounting of one on the back of an un-

Three views of the 8.8cm Flak 41 auf Sonderfahr-gestell.

Delivering orders to the crew of a Nashorn (Rhinoceros). The Nashorn was alternatively known as the Hornisse (Hornet). (Bundesarchiv).

14.12.43.

LP1615

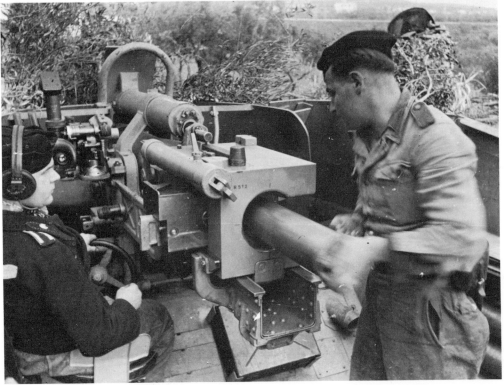

Side view of the Elefant mounting a Pak 43/2. Some of the Elefants which survived the Battle of Kursk were used in Italy.

Jagdpanther with a collared barrel for its Pak 43/3.

Loading the Pak 43/1 L/71 on a Nashorn. (Bundes-archiv).

Front view of the 8.8cm Pak 43/2 L/71 on the Panzer-jaeger Tiger P – the Elefant.

The ammunition lockers on a Nashorn. The vehicle carried a total of 40 rounds.

8.8cm Pak 43/3 auf Panzer-jaeger 38(t).

Pak 43/3 mounting in a Jagdpanther fighting compartment.

54

designated SdKfz 251 half-track variant in 1943. The gun was protected by a sloping shield and ammunition carried in a towed trailer. It is not known if this mounting was a serious experimental trial vehicle or whether the combination was purely intended as a display vehicle for an inspection by Hitler of the new Pak 43 guns.

One projected carriage for the Pak 43/3 was a self-propelled mounting on a Panzer IV chassis designated the Wg IV. With the gun mounted at the rear, in a manner similar to but lower than the Nashorn, the gun could traverse 30° and elevate from −4° to −13°. It did not leave the drawing board.

Another paper project was the mounting of an 8.8 cm. Flak 41 on a Panther chassis. The gun would have had full 360° traverse and the crew full protection in an armoured and enclosed turret. This project reached the wooden model stage but was stopped by the end of the war.

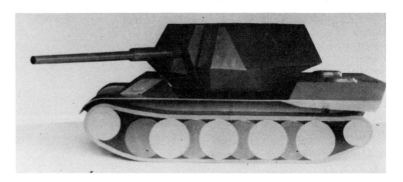

Data on Main 8.8 cm. Pak 43 Self-Propelled Vehicles.

	SdKfz 164 Nashorn	SdKfz 184 Elefant	SdKfz 173 Jagdpanther
Combat weight (tons)	24	68	45.5
Max. Speed by road (km./hr.)	40	20	46
Max. Speed across country (km./hr.)	24	10	24
Length overall (cm.)	844	814	986
Length without barrel (cm.)	580	680	687
Barrel overhang (cm.)	264	134	299
Width overall (cm.)	295	343	328
Height	265	297	272
Crew	5	6	5
Elevation	−5° to +20°	−6° to +14°	−8° to +14°
Traverse	30°	28°	22°

The Rigidly Mounted '88'

During 1943 work was started to produce a self-propelled gun which would not require a recoil mechanism. This gun would not be a recoilless weapon but a conventional barrel rigidly mounted direct onto hull armour or chassis members. The work was carried out under the direction of a Professor Waninger who supervised work by Alkett, and later Rheinmetall. The main advantage of this idea was to reduce the number of man hours and raw material needed for production, the saving of maintenance time, and the extra space saved inside the vehicle could be used for ammunition stowage.

Early experiments were made using a captured Russian 12 cm. mortar mounted on a Wespe chassis. This was only a feasibility study as the experiments continued with a 7.5 cm. Pak 39 rigidly mounted on a Pz.Jäg.38(t) Hetzer. Experiments moved the gun to a central position on the front plate and the earlier gimbal design by Alkett was replaced by a Rheinmetall designed ball mounting. Alterations were made

Model of the projected 8.8cm Flak 41 mounting on a Panther chassis.

8.8cm Pak 43/3 auf Krupp/ Steyr Sfl.38(d).

Hitler and his entourage examine the 8.8cm KwK 43 auf mittlerer Schuetzen- panzerwagen at a special demonstration of the new 8.8cm guns. In the back- ground can be seen a Pak 43/41 and an elevated Pak 43.

to the gun control linkages and the vehicle was put into production by Skoda at Pilsen just as the war ended.

The success of the Hetzer mounting prompted Krupps to experiment with the 8.8 cm. Pak 43/3 (L/71) in the Jagdpanther. They proposed that the gun would have to be mounted further back than usual and that the gun's rear seating be kept constant with a powerful spring. The elevating bracket was to have been mounted on the turret floor plate. Work was continuing on this mounting when the end of the war stopped any further progress.

Railway Mountings

The Allied policy of concentrating its bomber forces on single target areas in turn had the effects of intensifying the material damage and overwhelming local defence measures. To help overcome this attack policy, one measure taken was to provide railway mountings for aircraft guns to 'follow' the attacking bombers round the Reich whenever their forces concentrated on one area, e.g. the Hamburg attacks and the 'Battle of the Ruhr'. These units, known as Eisenbahnflak were mounted on several types of converted or specially built railway wagons. One of the most

Geschuetzwagen III (Eisb.) schwere Flak.

Improvised truck mounting. The truck sides could be lowered to form an extension on which the outrigger arms could be dropped. (Bundesarchiv).

common specially built wagons was the Geschützwagen III (Eisb.) schwere Flak. This mounted a single 8.8 cm. gun with a '/2' mounting. It had drop sides and stabilising screw jacks, and lockers to carry 216 rounds though extra rounds could be carried in accompanying trucks.

Though the Geschützwagen was widely used there were many other different types of wagon used for the same purpose. Some large wagons carried two guns while some were converted from closed wagons rather than flat-bed wagons.

Also used were field conversions of normal cruciform carriage 8.8 cm. pieces with the side outrigger arms removed and the main carriage member bolted down onto standard unconverted flat-bed wagons.

Guns used for the above wagons were all of the Flak 18–37 family. German sources state that the Flak 41 was not used as a railway gun but pictorial evidence shows that at least one battery was converted to be mounted on railway wagons. From the pictorial evidence it would appear that this was a local 'lash-up' as the stabilisers used were only timber props and the overall appearance is that of a hurried stop-gap.

When in action, the railway batteries usually

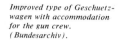

Improved type of Geschuetz-wagen with accommodation for the gun crew. (Bundesarchiv).

This type of Flakwagen mounted two 8.8cm Flak guns, the ammunition stowage being situated in the centre of the truck.

operated from marshalling yards or sidings. The gun crews lived on the train in converted carriages or goods wagons, which also contained all the offices, kitchens, workshops, etc. needed by a normal battery. Fire control equipment was also carried on the train. Some of the simpler field conversions lacked these refinements, but were often used in anti-partisan operations.

Experimental Guns

As the 8.8 cm. family was the most numerous of the heavy German anti-aircraft guns it is not surprising that there were a large number of research and experimental uses to which the guns were put. A list of these weapons would be long indeed, for there was hardly any field of armament research into which the Germans delved that did not involve the use of some item of 8.8 cm. equipment. A typical example of this is the research into the Peenemünde Pfiel Gescholl (PPG), a slender arrow-shaped shell intended for firing from a number of different calibre guns, but not intended for service use with the 8.8 cm. series. However, some 8.8 cm. barrels were used for experiments on the eventual shape of the involved sabot design needed for this new projectile. Both smooth-bored and rifled barrels appear to have been used, but the first PPG intended for service would have been used on the 10.5 cm. Flak 38 and 39. The war ended just as the design was ready for service trials.

Another experimental use involving ammunition was the research into the rifling used with sabot shells. Sabot ammunition involves the use of a sub-calibre shell fitting a full size barrel with a 'collar' or sabot to 'make up' to the full calibre. When fired the smaller projectile will have a higher muzzle velocity and thus greater range as the sabot collar falls away once the shell leaves the muzzle. Any instability in the smaller shell was corrected by the German designers by using rifling with increasing twist towards the muzzle, giving more stabilising spin to the shell. Work on these shells started in 1941 after scrutiny of experimental work in captured French establishments and all research was originally directed towards field and anti-tank artillery uses. In 1944, research was directed towards improving the 10.5 cm. Flak 38/39 and work was carried on by Krupps, Rheinmetall and Bochumer Verein. The result was a 10.5/8.8 cm. shell, reached after investigation into a wide range of experimental projectiles, to be fired from standard barrels. A similar shell for the 8.8 cm. Flak 36/37 emerged as an 8.8/7.2 cm. or 8.8/7.0 cm. shell after trials beginning in the Autumn of 1944. The guns used for these trials used both normal and increased twist rifling but the experiments were not completed by the end of the war. It was realised that the 7.2 or 7.0 cm. shell could have only a small HE filling but as a percussion fuse was to be fitted this would matter little.

Early research into remote control laying and loading of anti-aircraft guns led to the 8.8 cm. Flak J series. These were design studies started in 1933 under the control of the H.W.A. and involving, as usual, Krupps and Rheinmetall along with S.A.M. (Siemens Apparate unde Maschinen, who specialised in fire control equipment). Two prototypes were built based on the Flak 18, one using a purely electrical system and the other an electric/hydraulic system, and both involved remote laying by handwheels. Trials of the two systems started at Unterluss in

This simple railway mounting for a Flak 18 was made by removing the front and rear outrigger arms and bolting the main platform to the wagon floor.

1935 and the electric/hydraulic system was found to be more accurate and less prone to transit damage. This system was later fitted to the 10.5 cm. Flak 38, 12.8 cm. Flak 40 and 5.5 cm. Gerät 58. The same system was intended for the later 15 cm. Gerät 60 and 65.

Another experimental use of the 8.8 cm. gun was into research on the separate chamber system intended for the 24 cm. Gerät 80, development of which started in 1941 but was suspended in 1943. The massive Gerät 80 anti-aircraft gun was a Krupp project using a 23.8 cm. shell which, using normal fixed Q.F. rounds would introduce a lengthy and awkward shell and cartridge case combination with attendant handling, ramming and rate of fire problems. The Krupp answer was first suggested by a German Navy engineer who proposed that two propellent chambers be placed beside and parallel with the gun chamber, with all three chambers incorporated into the breech ring. Three breech blocks would also double as rammers, with normal breech loading sealing (obturation). The design conferred the following advantages:—

1) Three-piece ammunition would make for easier handling.
2) The extra chambers would put more weight at the breech and thus partially compensate for the inherent nose-heaviness of the long barrels involved.
3) The barrel would be shorter as the side chambers were no longer included in the overall length.
4) A shorter ram, as the ammunition parts were shorter and the breech blocks were themselves the rammers, thus increasing the possible rate of fire.

The new design impressed G.L. Flak who, like most gunners, were conservative enough to order trials with an existing gun. Accordingly an 8.8 cm. barrel was designed to incorporate the new chambers and was being built when the whole 24 cm. gun project was cancelled in November 1943.

Two 8.8 cm. naval guns were built by Krupp for experimental purposes. Both involved variations on the low recoil theme and only one of each appears to have been built. One, firing normal projectiles along a rifled bore, used double concentric chambers with exhaust ports forward of the cartridge case mouth. Due to the large mass of escaping gas a relatively large charge was needed, and a muzzle brake was fitted. Although the correct designation of this gun is not known brief details follow:—

Projectile weight	9 kg.	19.8 lbs.
Charge weight	2.8 kg.	6.2 lbs.
Muzzle velocity	595 m./sec.	1952 ft./sec.
Service pressure	1250 kg./sq. cm.	79 tons/sq. in.
Length	42 calibres	

The design of the other gun, the DUKA M-43 (Dusenkanone M-43), was started in 1943 and followed conventional recoilless gun practice. It was abandoned for naval use, probably due to the shipboard limitations imposed by the considerable backblast produced on firing. Brief details follow:—

Projectile weight	9 kg.	19.8 lbs.
Charge weight	1.6 kg.	3.5 lbs.
Muzzle velocity	600 m./sec.	1968 ft./sec.
Service pressure	2500 kg./sq. cm.	15.9 tons/sq. in.
Length	30 calibres	

Developed from the DUKA M-43 was an airborne version, sometimes referred to as the 8.8 cm. DUKA 88. Weighing 1000 kg. complete, it was 39 calibres (2560 mm) long and was designed for installation in a projected Junkers JU.88 ground attack variant to follow on from the JU.88P-4. Intended mainly for attacking large bomber formations (Pulkzerstörer) and also as an anti-tank weapon the DUKA 88 got as far as the prototype stage. Trials were held at Trueberg, East Prussia, with the gun suspended beneath a Junkers Ju87C-O. During 1944 the gun made some airborne firings but eventually an ammunition malfunction damaged the aircraft and the trials were discontinued.

The above mentioned weapons by no means cover the entire range of 8.8 cm. experimental guns but merely mentions some of the more important. Ammunition development is covered in the appropriate section.

Some Carriage Variants
Just as successful in its field as the 8.8 cm. Flak 18 was the gun's carriage, the cruciform (kreuzlafette) platform and pedestal. Originally developed for the unsuccessful 7.5 cm. Flak L/60, it

was progressively improved on the 8.8 cm. Flak 36 but remained basically the same as its designers originally intended. On the later Flak 41 and Gerät 42 the cruciform platform was retained but the pedestal was replaced by a turntable which made for a lower silhouette and easier hand loading. However, the basic Flak 18/37 carriage layout was retained for the 10.5 cm. Flak 38/39 and also for some heavier guns such as the heavier 15 cm. Gerät 50 and 55.

When mobile, the original Flak 18 was carried on two single axle bogies. Experience in Spain altered this simple arrangement into the Sonderhanger 201 and later into the Sonderhanger 202, both of which allowed the gun to be fired from its wheels. As a rare example of standardisation in the German ordnance arrangements, the same Sonderhanger 201 or 202 bogies were also used to transport the individual 8.8 cm. battery's own

Flak 18 on a Geschuetzwagen III. The crew appear to be handling blank rounds.

predictor and fire control equipment, the Kommandergerät 36 or 40.

The cruciform carriage was not used for the guns intended for a purely static anti-aircraft defence role. These guns were all suffixed '/2' as the Flak 18/2, Flak 36/2, Flak 37/2 and Flak 41/2. For these guns the pedestal mounting was bolted down or secured in a concrete bed, and transport to the sites was provided on a Sonderhänger 205. By late 1944 many of these static sites were being overrun with the resultant loss of their precious emplaced weapons for the simple reason there was no means of transporting them. In a belated attempt to provide some measure of tactical mobility for static guns an order for 4000 of the original cruciform carriages was put out to German industry on 5th January 1945. These were intended for use with a wide variety of weapons in addition to the 8.8 cm. guns but by the time the order was given, there was no hope of so many carriages ever being made, let alone delivered.

As well as providing a good mounting for the 8.8 cm. guns the pedestal was used for other purposes. One was as the mounting for a naval dual purpose anti-aircraft/coast defence gun, developed from a standard ship mounted weapon. Developed by Rheinmetall in 1938/39 this piece had what was probably the longest designation ever given to a gun since its full title was the '10.5 cm. Sk C/32 nL in 8.8 cm. MPL C/30 mit Deckenschutzshield'. The long title was probably the gun's only outstanding item of note for it had a rather indifferent performance in its dual role. The Deckenschutzshield was a cupola-type naval housing mounted on the pedestal and also on spring mounted rollers running on a track situated round the static emplacement. Proof only against splinters or small-arms fire, the cupola was probably of more use as a weather shield. Built in some numbers this 10.5 cm. ship's gun (SK) was installed round the coastline of the German 'Reich', but should not be confused with the totally different 10.5 cm. Flak 38 or 39.

The Flak 36 carriage was also intended for use with an anti-aircraft rocket launcher designed and built by the Czech firm of Skoda in about mid-1944. Mounted on the pedestal were 16 rocket rails each firing a 10.5 cm. solid fuel rocket weighing 19 kg. Construction of the launcher was simple and cheap since nearly all parts were made from angle iron. The layer was enclosed in a metal cabin mounted on the right of the launcher and similar launchers had been developed for ship and tank mountings but the whole project seems to have been accorded only a low priority. Brief details of the Flak 36 carriage-mounted launcher were as follows:—

Weight of rocket	19 kg.
Muzzle velocity	700 m./sec. (approx.)
Rail length	3500 mm.
Elevation	−3° to +85°
Traverse	360°
Weight in firing position	7000 kg. (approx.)
Indirect fire control	By predictor
Direct fire	By telescope

The Flak 36 carriage was also adapted to become the launcher for the Enzian (Gentian) guided surface-to-air missile. For this purpose the carriage was altered only by the omission of fire control and fuse setting equipment and the barrel replaced by two 6.8 m. (22′ 4″) long angle iron launching rails. The missile, based on the aerodynamics of the Me163 rocket interceptor, was intended for use against large bomber formations and had a service ceiling of 41,000 ft. Designed by a Dr. Wurster of Messerschmitt in early 1944 the missile was built of laminated wood and guided by a radio link from a ground joystick control. There were five different models, only four of which were built, but of the 38 missiles tested only a few came anyway near to meeting the design specification. As a result the project was dropped in January 1945. Wing span was 4 metres (13′ 1½″) and length was 2.4 metres (7′ 10½″). Weight, including four take-off boost-

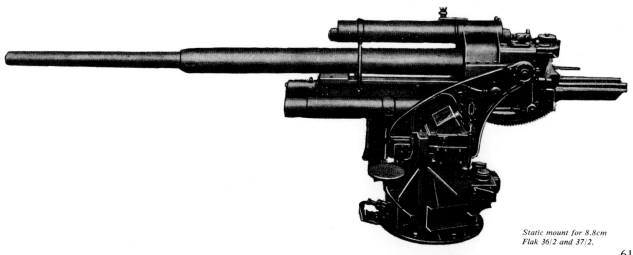

Static mount for 8.8cm Flak 36/2 and 37/2.

ers, was 1800 kg. (3969 lbs.).

Another surface-to-air missile associated with the 8.8 cm. carriage was the Rheintochter (Rhine-daughter, or Rhine-maiden). This time the launching carriage was that for the Flak 41 which was virtually unchanged except for the substitution of a short launching rail for the gun – even the shield was retained. Rheintochter was a more sophisticated and advanced project than Enzian, and was designed by Rheinmetall-Borsig, who received a development contract in November 1942. Work on the two-stage solid fuel missile proceeded rather slowly and by July 1944 only 34 had been test-fired, rising to 45 by September of that year. Three different models were projected but tests were still in progress when the war ended. Length of the intended operational version, the R-IIIf, was 5 m. (16′ 5″) and launch weight was approximately 1500 kg. (3307 lbs.). It did not see operational service.

Yet another Rheinmetall-Borsig missile that used a modified Flak 41 carriage was the result of extensive research by Rheinmetall and could be fired from either an A4 (V-2) transporter or from a much modified Flak 41 carriage. This was Rheinbote, a long range bombardment missile. Maximum range that could be achieved was 218 km. (136 miles) due to the vehicle's three stage construction (plus take-off booster). However, the total take-off weight of 1715 kg. (3775 lb.) could deliver a warhead of only 40 kg. (88 lb.) which could be of only nuisance or propaganda value. Unlike many other rocket projects, Rheinbote did see action for it was used to bombard Antwerp in November 1944. Over 200 were fired from Zwolle in Holland, each of which reached a height of some 78 km. (48.5 miles) and a speed reaching Mach 5.5. Overall length was 11.4 m. (37′ 4⅞″), and at its widest part – the take-off booster – Rheinbote measured only 53.5 cm. (1′ 9″).

One further Flak rocket in the development stage that was intended for use with a 8.8 cm. carriage (type unspecified) was the unguided Taifun (Typhoon). This, unlike the other rockets mentioned above, was an unguided missile developed at the Elektromechanische Werke (ENW) at Peenemunde. Using two self-igniting liquid fuels, Taifun had a very rapid take-off and was intended for near-vertical ripple launching at large bomber formations. It had an 0.5 kg. warhead and was 1.93 metres (6′ 4″) long. Weight was 21 kg. (46.2 lbs.) and operational height was 15 km. (9.3 miles).

The number of rockets carried on rails by the converted 8.8 cm. carriages is quoted in one source as 30 and in another as 46. Optimistic production forecasts of 2 million a month from mid-1945 on were made to supply 400 batteries each of 12 projectors, but in February 1945, Peenemünde was abandoned to the advancing Red Army and incomplete development work could not be resumed in time elsewhere.

Although separate and entirely different from

the usual 8.8 cm. carriage, the improvised carriage of the 8.8 cm. Pak 43/41 followed general field artillery practice. It was, however, heavy and had a tendency to sink into soft ground when fired. To help overcome this, a light pedestal mount for securing under the carriage axle to spread the weight over a greater ground area was developed by Skoda at Pilsen. Known as the 'Scheisstutze für Pak-Geräte und leichte Feldgeschutze', it was also intended for use with the 7.5 cm. Pak 40, 10.5 cm. 1e F.H.18 and 10.5 cm. 1e F.H.18/40.

AMMUNITION

Ammunition for the 8.8 cm. guns can be divided into three main groups. First comes the ammunition for the Flak 18, 36 and 37 and the KwK 36. Then comes the ammunition for the Flak 41, and a further group for the Pak 43, its derivatives, and the KwK 43. All used similar shells but the cartridge cases varied in size. The case for the

10.5cm rail type rocket launcher mounted on an 8.8cm Flak carriage.

10.5cm rocket launcher in firing position.

Flak 41 was longer than that for the Flak 18/37 while the Pak 43 case was shorter and fatter than that for the Flak 41. These size variations were to accommodate the increased loads for higher muzzle velocities and improved performance.

Basically, 8.8 cm. rounds were fixed, or Q.F. rounds, with the shell and cartridge joined together, handled and loaded in one piece. While this had the advantages of easy supply and speed in loading, handling the bulky combination was no easy task, especially when hand loading with the gun firing in the horizontal position. Also using a metal cartridge case for breech obturation (sealing) was rather costly in raw materials. One of the main supply difficulties for the Germans was the relative shortage of copper and thus brass, used for the early cartridge cases. To overcome this drawn steel cases were introduced after a brief attempt to use brass plated steel cases. Rounds were supplied to the gun in flat wood and wicker boxes each containing three rounds or packed singly in steel tubes, sealed against moisture and dust.

Early 8.8 cm. cartridges used cordite for the main propellent. This material considerably shortened barrel life and was soon replaced by Diglycol, a material made up of nitrocellulose and sthylene glycoldinate. Further improvements led to the introduction of Gudol which was Diglycol with the addition of nitroguanidine, which considerably reduced barrel erosion and wear. Primers could be either of the C/12 nA percussion variety or C/22 for electrical firing, depending on the gun for which the round was

An Enzian missile ready for launching from its adapted Flak 36 mounting.

Like a series of still frames from the old Zoetrope this photograph shows ammunition being delivered to a Flak 18 site. Each man carries three rounds in a wood and wicker container. Note the partially buried data transmission cable.

intended. Cartridge cases were clearly marked with the type of guns with which they could be used.

The main differences between the two types of cartridge cases for anti-aircraft use can be seen from the following list:—

	Flak 18 – 37	Flak 41
Length	568 mm.	880 mm.
Mouth diameter	90.5 mm.	90.5 mm.
Shoulder diameter	96.7 mm.	105 mm.
Rim Diameter	102 mm.	123 mm.
Weight	5.28 kg.	6.08 kg.

The shells used in all main types of gun were basically similar and can be divided into two main groups – H.E. (Sprenggranate) and armour piercing (Panzergranate), with hollow charge, grooved shells and starshells making up smaller groups. Each shell was designated as to whether it was nose fuzed (Kopfzündung or Kz.) or base fuzed (Bodenzunder or Bd.z.), the latter being used mainly with A.P. rounds. For the nose fuzed H.E. rounds, time fuzes were used but by the end of the war these fuzes incorporated a percussion element. This percussion element was introduced after experimental work had proved that a direct hit on a four-engined heavy bomber would need as little as 400 grams of H.E. filling to bring it down while a much larger air-bursting charge was needed to produce the same result. The time fuzes used in 8.8 cm. ammunition were produced mainly by Thiel who made standard clockwork fuzes and Junghaus who produced centrilfugal weight operated fuzes. The direct action percussion fuze was incorporated into both of these types by Skoda.

Early 8.8 cm. shells used copper driving bands but as has already been mentioned, copper was one of Germany's most sensitive raw material bottlenecks. To overcome this shortage, sintered iron bands were developed by the Kaiser-Wilhelm-Gesellschaft of Dusseldorf under the trade name of Weichstahl. Shells incorporating these bands carried the extra designation FES. The

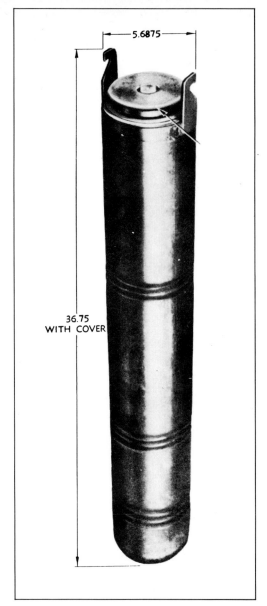

Individual cartridge carton for a Flak 18/37 round.

Components of an 8.8cm Sprenggranate Patrone L/4.5 (Kz).

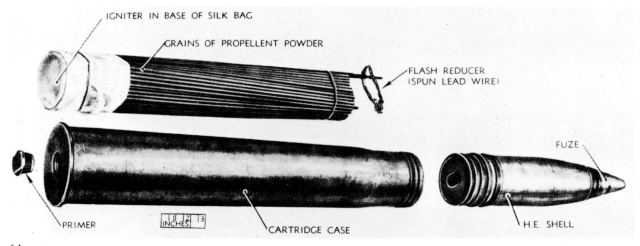

IGNITER IN BASE OF SILK BAG

GRAINS OF PROPELLENT POWDER

FLASH REDUCER (SPUN LEAD WIRE)

FUZE

PRIMER

INCHES

CARTRIDGE CASE

H.E. SHELL

sintered iron (Sintereisen) bands had the added advantage of producing less barrel wear and were a significant factor in prolonging barrel life.

In an attempt to improve shell fragmentation in air bursts some shells were grooved longitudinally. These grooves, usually about 15, were about 4 mm. deep and were introduced after study of captured Russian A.A. ammunition in 1941. Introduced as a stop-gap measure until more efficient fragmentation shells, described in the section on experimental ammunition, could be developed, these rounds carried the extra designation 'Gerillt' or grooved.

Listed below are the main types of 8.8 cm. ammunition. The list should not be thought of as complete but is the most comprehensive listing that can be compiled at the time of writing.

8.8 cm. Sprenggranate Patrone L/4.5 (Kz) (HE)
For Flak 18, 36, 37.
Shell weight 9.24 kg.
Charge 0.86 kg. Amatol 40/60
Fuze A.Z. 23/28 or Zt/Z S/3.
Shell colour yellow or green.
Similar: 8.8 cm. Sprenggranate Patrone Kwk 43.

8.8 cm. Panzergranate Patrone 39 (APCBC)
For Flak 18, 36, 37, 39 (r) and Kwk 36.
Shell weight 10 kg.
Charge 114 grams Cyclonite/wax.
Fuze Bd.Z 5103 or 103/1.
Shell colour black or black with red markings.
Similar: 8.8 cm. Panzergranate Patrone 39/1 Flak 41.
        8.8 cm. Panzergranate Patrone 39 Flak 41.
        8.8 cm. Panzergranate Patrone 39–1 Kwk 43.
The 'standard' anti-tank round.

8.8 cm. Panzergranate Patrone 40 (AP)
For Flak 36, 41, Kwk 36, 43, Pak 43.
Shell weight 7.27 kg.
Tungsten core (solid).
Shell colour black.
Similar: 8.8 cm. Panzergranate Patrone 40 Flak 41.
        8.8 cm. Panzergranate Patrone 40/43 Kwk 43.
One of the tungsten cored 'AP40' family of projectiles used in all German anti-tank guns.

8.8 cm. Panzergranate Patrone (mit Bd.Z.)
For Flak 18, 36, 37.
Shell weight 9.44 kg.
Charge 131 grams TNT/Wax.
Fuze Bd.ZF. 8.8 cm. Pzgr.
Shell colour black.

8.8 cm. Sprengranate Patrone L/4.5 (gerillt) (HE)
For Flak 18, 36, 37, Kwk 36.
Shell weight 9.54 kg.
Charge 0.91 kg. poured Amatol 40/60.
Fuze Zt.Z. S/30.
Shell colour yellow with black markings.
Grooved shell for improved fragmentation.

8.8 cm. Hohlladung Granate 39 (Gr.39HL) (HEAT)
For Kwk 36, 43, Pak 43 & 43/41.
Shell weight 7.65 kg.
Charge 0.91 kg. pressed Cyclonite/wax.
Fuze AZ.38.
Shell colour olive drab.
Similar: 8.8 cm. Panzergranate Patrone 39HL Kwk 43.
        8.8 cm. Panzergranate Patrone 39/43 HL Kwk 43.
A hollow charge shell which despite its success was not able to realise its full potential due to the high shell velocity and speed of rotation. The hollow charge effect is best used on slow-moving projectiles such as that fired from the 8.8 cm. Panzerschreck rocket launchers.

8.8 cm. Sprenggranate Patrone L/4.7 (FES)
For Flak 41.
Shell weight 9.4 kg.
Charge 0.86 kg. Amatol 40/60.
Fuze AZ 23/28 or Zt.Z. S/30.
Shell colour yellow.
(FES) refers to the use of sintered iron driving bands. Used a brass case.

8.8 cm. Sprenggranate Patrone 43 KwK 43 (HE)
For KwK 43, Pak 43, 43/41.
Shell weight 9.4 kg.
Charge 1 kg. poured Amatol 40/60.
Fuze AZ 23/28 or Dopp.Z.
Shell colour olive drab.

8.8 cm. Panzergranate 39/43 KwK 43 (HEAT)
For KwK 43, Pak 43, 43/41.
Shell weight 10.16 kg.
Charge 137 grams Cyclonite/wax.
Fuze Bd.Z.5127.
Black with red markings.

8.8 cm. Leichtgranate Patrone L/4.4 (Kz) (Starshell)
For Flak 18, 36, 37, 41, 39 (r).
Shell weight 9.3 kg.
Fuze Zt.Z. S/60 na A.Zn.
Shell colour light green with black tip.
Used for target illumination, but also as a navigation aid or marker, this starshell incorporated an illuminated container which was ejected from the shell and suspended on a 22" diameter parachute. The 'star' container could burn for about 23 seconds and had an intensity of 375,000 candlepower.

To the above list can be added drill rounds for practically every round mentioned, and blanks for exercises and saluting purposes.

8.8 cm. rounds were also used as sub-calibre ammunition (with sabots) for the 10.5 cm. 1e F.H.18 field gun (as the 10.5 cm. Sprgn. 42TS),

This photograph from the Aberdeen Proving Grounds in the United States, shows clearly the physical differences between the three main types of 8.8cm ammunition. From the left the rounds are for:
A. Flak 18, 36, 37, and KwK 36.
B. Flak 41.
C. Pak 43 group, KwK 43.

10.5 cm. Flak 38 and 39 and 10.5 cm. Flak 40/39 (a 12.8 cm. Flak 40 barrel lined down to 10.5 cm.). In the latter application a 9.4 kg. shell could attain a muzzle velocity of 4400 ft./second, but the idea does not appear to have seen other than field trials.

8.8 cm. Fuzes – a summary

A.Z. 23/28	Nose fuze. Could be adjusted for immediate action or 0.1 sec. delay.
A.Z. 38	Nose fuze. Impact.
Zt.Z. S/30	Nose fuze. Clockwork time action up to 30 secs. (adjustable). Made by Thiel.
Zt.Z. S/30 Fgl.	Nose fuze. Centrifugal weight action. Variable up to 30 secs. Made by Junghaus.
Dopp.Z.	Nose fuze. Clockwork. Fixed time delays of 60, 90 or 160 secs. for producing above-ground airbursts in long-range field artillery roles.
Bd.Zf. 8.8 cm. Pzgr.	Base fuze. Available in two sizes. A percussion fuze it could be varied to provide a delay to allow the HEAT shell to explode inside a vehicle.
Bd.Z. 5127	Base fuze. Variable as Bd.Zf. 8.8 cm. Pzgr.
Bd.Z.5103 & 5103/1	Base fuze. Variable.

Experiments were made with rudimentary radio and acoustic proximity fuzes, electric time and combustion fuzes but none left the development stage. Consideration was also given to photo-electric fuzes for use against searchlight illuminated aircraft but the project was dropped.

Experimental Ammunition

As has already been mentioned in the section on experimental guns, the Germans carried out a great deal of research work into sub-calibre projectiles involving the use of sabot liners. The idea behind this research was to be able to boost the performance of existing guns without the time lag and expense involved in producing new weapons. Smaller projectiles fired from existing barrels would have an increased muzzle velocity and thus be able to reach greater altitudes in less time. Both discarding sabot and skirted, or flanged, projectiles were tried with variable riflings and the range of experiments are best summarised in tabular form. Only the experiments involving 8.8 cm. shells are mentioned – there were numerous other experimental combinations in other calibres.

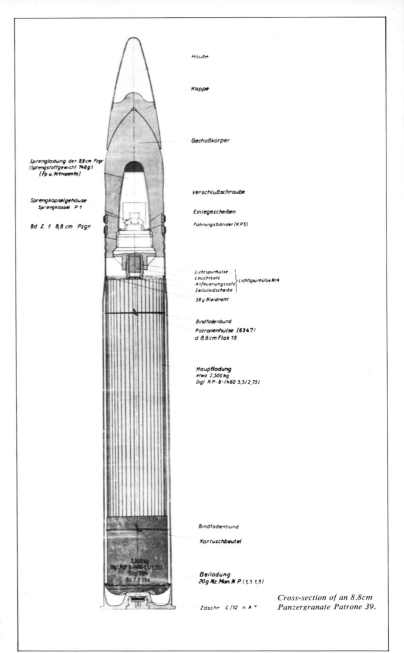

Cross-section of an 8.8cm Panzergranate Patrone 39.

	Calibre of projectile (cm.)	Type of projectile	Length of projectile (calibres)	Weight of projectile (kg.)	Muzzle velocity (m./s.)
8.8 cm. Flak 18, 36, 37	8.8/7.0	DS–HE	4.2	5.1/4.4	1085
	8.8/7.0	Skirted–HE	4.1	4.4	1195
8.8 cm. Flak 41	8.8/7.0	DS–HE	4.2	5.1/4.4	1290
	8.8/7.0	Skirted–HE	4.1	4.4	1360
10.5 cm. Flak 38, 39	10.5/8.8	DS–HE	4.1	10.8/9.0	1065
	10.5/8.8	DS–Inc. Shr.	4.1	11.0/9.2	2060
	10.5/8.8	Skirted–HE	4.0	9.3	1130
	10.5/8.8	Skirted–Inc. Shr.	4.1	9.3	1130
10.5 cm. Flak 40/39	10.5/8.8	DS–Inc. Shr.	4.4	10.2/8.8	1340

Ds = Discarding Sabot.
Inc. Shr. = Brandschrapnell.

All the above shells used percussion fuzes. In addition to the above, development of an 8.8/7.2 cm. sabot shell was in progress as the war ended.

Mention has already been made of the 'Gerillt' shell as an attempt to improve shell fragmentation. Krupps experimented with a 'Granatschrapnell' shell with a similar objective but this projectile was a return to the original concept of the 'spherical case' shell evolved by Lt. Henry Shrapnel back in 1784. As then, the Granatschrapnell was a HE shell packed with solid steel pellets. However, these pellets were designed to be projected forward prior to the shell being exploded by a delay fuze. Later, the pellets were intended to be filled with an incendiary compound as the 'Fla. Sprgr.'.

A Rheinmetall design similar to the above was 'Brand-Sprenggranate' which existed in two forms. One projected the 72 incendiary percussion fuzed pellets forward at a 30f included angle and another outwards. Composition of these pellets was barium nitrate – 48 %, magnesium alloy – 24.6 %, aluminium alloy – 24.6 % and residue – 2.8 %. This complex and expensive shell was used operationally on a small scale with Flak 18, 36 and 37 anti-aircraft units as the Granate Brand Schrapnell Flak. Shells weighed 9.1 kg. and contained an 0.1 kg. TNT or Amatol/wax bursting charge. A Zt.Z. S/30 fuse was fitted and the shells were colour coded with a blue body, red ogive and green tip.

An idea which attracted anti-aircraft designers on both sides of the World War II conflict was the aerial mine. This was an explosive device suspended in the path of bomber formations by a small parachute. A design started by G.L. Flak was handed over to Krupps in 1940 and was designated the 'D. Geschoss'. Carried to altitude inside a special 8.8 cm. shell, an ejection charge blew out the mine under the control of a time fuze, after which the shell case was fragmented by a small nose charge. Tests during 1941 and 1942 showed the difficulties inherent in such a complex and expensive device and the idea was dropped during 1943.

THE '88' IN ACTION

Although designed as an anti-aircraft gun the 8.8 cm. family really made its mark as a dual-purpose weapon. When employed as an anti-tank weapon during the early war years its performance both in range and armour penetration placed it far ahead of any other anti-tank weapon in service elsewhere. Its performance as an anti-aircraft gun was also good, but by the closing years of the war the Flak 18/37 group was in danger of becoming obsolescent with the advent of the high-speed, high-altitude bomber. Despite this it remained the mainstay of the anti-aircraft defences of the German Reich and was in service in greater numbers than any other heavy Flak weapon.

Anti-Aircraft

Ideally, the '88' was intended for anti-aircraft use from a fixed and prepared site. To this end the already mentioned '/2' guns were delivered with pedestal mounts only and by 1943, three-quarters of all 88 production was turned out in this form. This had the resultant saving of material resources since tractors, limbers and cruciform carriages were not required for these guns, but it did mean the expenditure of vast amounts of concrete and labour in the erection of fixed gun emplacements.

The wood and wicker basket used for storage and delivery of rounds to the guns.

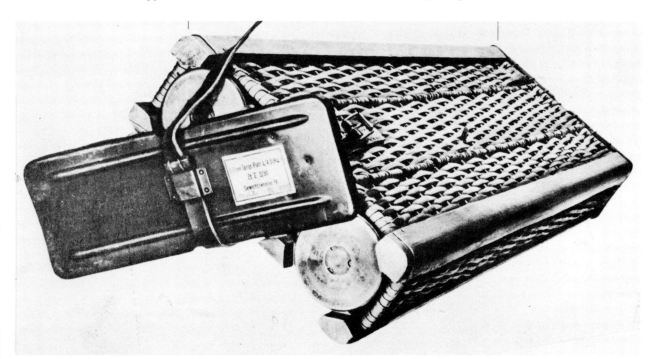

Also, these fixed sites were often found to be a liability since the Allied Air Forces usually attacked targets in rotation with all their bomber strength concentrating on one target at any one time. Thus it often happened that many fixed sites were presented with targets only infrequently while the defences of others were overwhelmed by sheer weight of numbers. This inflexibility of the fixed site was partially overcome by the use of railway batteries but the ideal answer was the mobile road battery used by the Army formations. Defence of the Reich was a Luftwaffe responsibility.

The divisions of defence responsibilities between the Wehrmacht and Luftwaffe was a constant source of friction between the two especially where allotment of 8.8 cm. guns from the production lines was concerned. However, this friction extended right down the chain of command to battery level. It was not unknown for Luftwaffe guns allotted to anti-aircraft defence to be 'appropriated' by Army commands for use as anti-tank guns. Where the guns concerned were of the Flak 37 variety this meant that they became virtually useless as Flak weapons since the control gear was often removed and replaced by direct fire sighting arrangements. At a higher level the influence of Goering usually

meant that the Luftwaffe defence units and field divisions got their full complement of weapons, with the Wehrmacht units getting only what was left.

The full complement for a mobile gun of the Flak 18–37 series was 11 men with the Flak 41 detachment employing 12. (7.62/8.8 cm. Flak 39 (r) detachments also used 11 men.) Of the 11 gun numbers, nine actually served the gun with the other two numbers being, one the detachment commander and the other the driver of the towing vehicle – usually a Sd.Kfz. 7. Their duties were as follows:—

No. 1	Layer for elevation
No. 2	Layer for line (traverse)
No. 3	Loader
No. 4	Ammunition number
No. 5	Ammunition number
No. 6	Fuze setting mechanism operator
No. 7	Fuze setter (putting round into machine)
No. 8	Ammunition number
No. 9	Ammunition number

On the Flak 41 an extra man assisted in elevation control. On static sites the number of men to a crew was smaller, usually only seven, but early in the war the number to a gun was nine. The 8.8 cm. guns were all able to bring down a heavy bomber such as the Lancaster or B-17

An early 8.8cm Flak 18 on tow behind a semi-armoured Mittlerer Zugkraftwagen 8t during the German advance through France, 31 May 1940.

A Luftwaffe No. 3 hand-loading a round.

A cold sentry piquet guarding a Flak 18.

Anti-Tank

For all its success as an anti-tank gun the Flak 18/36 was not primarily designed for the role and was only used as such because of circumstances forced upon the Wehrmacht. In 1940 and '41 the British Matilda tank held sway over the battlefields of North Africa by virtue of its heavy frontal armour which could not be pierced by the anti-tank guns then available. The two 'standard' Pak guns, the 3.7 cm. Pak 35/36 and 5 cm. Pak 38 were both too light for the task and heavier field guns lacked the A.P. ammunition needed. The result was that the 8.8 cm. guns were forced to take on the job of tackling the heavy British armour and fell back on the limited experience gained in action against the light tanks encountered in the Spanish Civil War.

In the desert, however, the 8.8 cm. guns really came into their own. The flat terrain enabled the '88's' to take advantage of their prime asset – range. Tanks encountering the emplaced guns were fired on at ranges far in excess of that which could be usefully countered by their own armament, and at upwards of 2000 yards their armour could be pierced and the vehicles destroyed. As an extra morale depressant the first intimation (and last) that an Allied tank crew often had of the presence of an '88' was a shell exploding *inside* their vehicle due to the delayed action of the base fuzed HEAT rounds. Time and time again, the '88's' wreaked havoc in tank attacks, and even after the Eighth Army had learned to be wary of German feints that drew tanks on to carefully emplaced guns set in ambush, the '88' gathered a fresh harvest in Tunisia. In their first encounters with the '88', the green American armour units suffered heavy losses, especially during the battles of the Kasserine Pass. Again, in Russia the '88' often saved the day against massed Russian tank assaults.

But for all its successes, the 8.8 cm. Flak 18 and 36 was not ideally suited to its anti-tank role. For one thing it was high, bulky and difficult to conceal. For ideal protection it required a large amount of effort to dig in and conceal. When pressed into action in the open the crew were very vulnerable to small arms and artillery fire. Even the addition of a shield (some with hinged sides) could not protect the crew from air bursts. As a precautionary measure therefore the crews had to become experts in getting their guns in and out of action in a very short time. In this they were helped by the introduction into service of the Sonderhänger 202 which meant that the gun barrel faced away from the tractor, i.e. to the rear. This was of considerable assistance in speedy withdrawals from action.

As well as being used as an anti-tank gun the Flak 18 and 36 were also used on occasion as field pieces. This was rather a waste of their potential but their range was often useful to shell rear assembly and storage areas with time fuzed HE shells. When this occurred the fuze setter abandoned his machine and set the fuzes by

8.8cm Flak 18.

Flying Fortress with a single shell, but this 'hit' had to be a 'near-miss' air burst since the HE (Sprenggranate) shells relied on time fuzes and did not have any direct action percussion fuzes until the last year of the war. Thus the accuracy of the weapons was very dependent on the accuracy of the information from the control predictors or radar, and the time lag (dead time) spent in relaying the control information to the guns. This dead time was reduced to a practical minimum on the Flak 41 by the use of fuze setting mechanism on the loading tray but most other guns had to rely on external fuze setters. The introduction, albeit on a small scale, of incendiary shrapnel shells greatly increased the efficiency of the earlier guns.

The increase in performance of the Flak 41 over earlier models meant that special consideration was given to its siting round targets of prime importance in the Reich. After early experiments in North Africa as an anti-tank gun the Flak 41 was devoted almost exclusively to the Flak role. A few were fitted on to Flak towers to give a full 360° coverage. An added advantage of a fixed emplacement for the Flak 41 was that full workshop and maintenance facilities could be laid on close by – in view of the frequent technical troubles generated by this complex weapon this was an important consideration.

hand. The layer had rather an unenviable task as the dial sight used in indirect artillery fire was mounted on top of the recuperator cylinder. To use it the layer had to clamber up over the gun and expose himself to any counter-battery fire that may have been directed against their positions.

The introduction of the 8.8 cm. Pak 43 overcame all of the difficulties encountered by earlier marks. Lower, well protected, and easy to conceal, as well as possessing a higher performance the new gun was a great and immediate success. It's stop-gap cousin, the 8.8 cm. Pak 43/41 was less of a success due to its large and clumsy bulk, but it possessed the same 'reach' and power of its more sophisticated relation and could thus take on any Allied tank.

When emplaced on vehicles, the only tactical

88s on tow.

Siebel ferries were used to transport equipment from Italy to North Africa. The cargo of this one includes an 8.8cm Flak 36 and a wireless truck.

A Flak 18 in action straight from its wheels in North Africa.

limitations imposed on the KwK 36 and 43 and the mobile Pak 43's were the performance limitations of their vehicles. This was particularly true of the Tiger I and II mountings. Both of these vehicles were so large and heavy that they were not sufficiently mobile to employ their weapons to their full effect. Perhaps the most effective mobile carriage for the 8.8 cm. family was the Jagdpanther mounting the 8.8 cm. Pak 43/3. This carriage had only a limited traverse and was built in insufficient numbers to affect the course of the conflict.

8.8 cm. Gun Formations

Very broadly, organisation of 8.8 cm. gun units was divided between Luftwaffe and Wehrmacht commands, with the Luftwaffe units being primarily concerned with the defence of the Reich. Luftwaffe units will be considered first.

Largest of the Luftwaffe AA. units was the Flakdivision. Composition, equipment and numbers are shown in the accompanying table but it must be stressed that there were many variations to this establishment.

Following this is a breakdown of the equip-

A column of Second British Army Cromwells rumble past a captured Pak 43/41 in Normandy. Note the camouflage on the gun. (IWM)

A standard German propaganda shot of 88s in action.

▶

72

ment of a motorised anti-aircraft regiment, and of a Mixed anti-aircraft battalion (motorised).

All the above units are examples of the 8.8 cm. guns being used in defence of the Reich. There were many variations of these themes, e.g. static units had lower personnel strengths.

8.8 cm. guns were also used by Luftwaffe Railway Anti-Aircraft (Eisenbahnflak) units. These were grouped in regiments, each composed of three heavy battalions or two heavy and one light battalion. Each battalion had three or four batteries, usually with one battery allotted to a train.

Army unit 8.8 cm. strengths varied with the type of division to which they were allotted. These numbers refer to anti-aircraft and anti-tank guns combined.

Infantry Division	12
Motorised Division	8
Panzer Division	8
SS Panzer Division	12
Luftwaffe Parachute Division	12

These guns were allocated to Anti-Aircraft Battalions, and divided between two or three batteries of four guns each.

8.8 cm. anti-tank guns were usually allocated to Festungs-Pak Kompanies under a Festungs-Pak-Battalion, of which there were several in any Army Sector under the control of a local Festungs-Pak Verband. This answered direct to the local Army Command.

The above details relate only to 8.8 cm. gun organisations, and even among the few mentioned it must be stressed that there were many variations and other types of unit other than those mentioned.

8.8 cm. Gun Production

While total production numbers for the anti-tank gun versions are not available it is known that by late 1944 a total of 16,227 had been built. This total includes Flak 18, 36, 37 and 41 versions. Totals for 1945 are not available.

Production of the Flak 18 started at the Krupp plant at Essen but extra lines were soon opened elsewhere. The coming of the Allied bomber offensive bought about a disposal of assembly lines and a diversification of sub-contractors for parts and sub-assemblies. One line that was just beyond useful bomber range was established at the Skoda Works at Pilsen with a planned output of 200 Flak 36/37 guns per month. Production in March 1945 was actually 180, and the list of sub-contractors for major parts is shown below to illustrate the problems inherent in reaching

A battery of Flak 18 guns on the road.

planned production totals at a time when the transport system of the Reich was breaking down under constant air attack.

Parts/assemblies made by Skoda at Pilsen	Parts/sub assemblies supplied
Gun tubes	Tubes. Skoda, Dubrnica.
Breech	Breech. Schöller-Blackman, Ternitz.
	Receiver. Schöller-Blackman, Ternitz.
Breech parts	Parts. Rheinmetall-Borsig, Tegel.
Ejector mechanism	Parts. Andritz, Gratz.
Block mechanism	Parts. Andritz, Gratz.
Recoil mechanism	Moving parts. Gutberlet, Leipzig.
Traversing gear	Parts. Ruhrstall, Hattingen.
	Parts. Fischer, Nordhausen.
Pivot	Parts. Drettmann, Osterholz.
	Parts. Dornen, Dortmund.
	Parts. Wertheim, Wien.
Recuperator	Brake. Berglütte, Koln.
	Parts. MAN, Ausburg.
	Parts. Ruhrstall, Hattingen.
	Parts. Nileswerke, Siegmar.
Cradle	Parts. Voith, Heidenheim.
Equilibriators	Parts. Stahlwerke, Brunninghaus.
	Parts. Christgen, Dortmund.
Top gun carriage	Parts. Halberg, Ludwigshafen.
	Parts. Drettman, Osterholz.
	Rheinmetall-Borsig, Tegel.
	Elevation gear. Erlich, Gotha.
	Elevation gear. Zahnräderfabrik, Ausburg.
	Elevation gear. Heidenreich, Maburg.
	Height receiver. Gaspary, Markränstadt.
	Side receiver. Zahnräderfabrik, Ausburg.
	Fire control. Westfalmaschinenfabrik F., Recklinghausen.
	Fire setting gear. Flakzeugamt, Velten. Erhard, Frudenau.
	Cruciform carriage. Drettman, Osterholz. Waagner-Burg, Wien. Schumann-Werdau Kelle und Hildebrand, Niederseidlitz.
	Straightening mechanism. Rheinmetall-Borsig, Sömmerda.

8.8 cm. Gun Costs

The following costs of various 8.8 cm. weapons are quoted in a document dated 1.2.43. Unfortunately, at that time the Reichsmark was not convertible into Sterling or dollars so accurate comparisons cannot be made. The costs quoted do not include tractors, where applicable.

8.8 cm. Flak 18.	31,750RM.
8.8 cm. Flak 36.	33,600RM.
8.8 cm. Flak 41.	60,000RM.
8.8 cm. Pak 43/2.	20,000RM.
8.8 cm. Pak 43/3.	21,000 RM.
8.8 cm. KwK 36.	18,000RM.
8.8 cm. KwK 43.	21,000RM.

A captured Flak 36 or 37 taken by American troops in the Ardennes being towed behind an M4 Tractor – probably for use against its former owners, as the Americans were great believers in the re-use of captured equipment.

Firing on a practice range this 8.8cm Pak 43/41 has just scored a direct hit on a captured T34/76 on the brow of the ridge.

▼

ANTI-AIRCRAFT REGIMENT (MOTORISED)

	Officers	N.C.O.'s	Privates	Rifles	Pistols	Sub M.G.'s	L.M.G.'s	20 mm. AA.	20 mm. QUAD. AA.	8.8 cm. AA.	Vehicles	Motorcycles	60 cm. Searchlights
Regimental H.Q.	9	34	123	140	20	10	2				25	5	
Mixed AA. Battalion	39	403	908	1051	241	93	17	30	18	12	339	38	12
Mixed AA. Battalion	39	403	908	1051	241	93	17	30	18	12	339	38	12
Mixed AA. Battalion	39	403	908	1051	241	93	17	30	18	12	339	38	12
TOTALS	126	1243	2847	3293	743	289	53	90	54	36	1042	119	36

FLAKDIVISION

	Personnel	LMG's	20 mm. AA.	20 mm. QUAD. AA.	37 mm. AA.	8.8 cm. AA.	10.5 cm. AA.	60 cm. Searchlights	105 cm. Searchlights	200 cm. Searchlights	Barrage Balloons	Vehicles	Trailers	Motorcycles
Div. H.Q.	200	2										30	1	20
Air Defence Signal Battalion	300	11										44	12	10
Heavy Searchlight Regiment	2043	29							90	18		94	255	52
AA. Regiment	2448	38	52	9	12	24	16	16			72	109	238	55
AA. Regiment	2448	38	52	9	12	24	16	16			72	109	238	55
AA. Regiment	2448	38	52	9	12	24	16	16			72	109	238	55
Air Medical Unit	250	2										37		2
TOTALS	10137	158	156	27	36	72	48	48	90	18	216	532	982	249

MIXED ANTI-AIRCRAFT BATTALION (MOTORISED)

	Officers	N.C.O.'s	Privates	Rifles/Carbines	Pistols	Sub M.G.'s	L.M.G.'s	20 mm. AA.	20 mm. QUAD. AA.	8.8 cm. AA.	Vehicles	Motorcycles	60 cm. Searchlights
Battalion H.Q., Command Platoon	6	31	93	74	41	19	1				28	11	
8.8 cm. Battery	4	53	110	149	12	10	2	4		4	36	3	
8.8 cm. Battery	4	53	110	149	12	10	2	4		4	36	3	
8.8 cm. Battery	4	53	110	149	12	10	2	4		4	36	3	
20 mm. Battery*	6	65	139	151	51	14	2	9	3		58	5	4
20 mm. Battery	6	65	139	151	51	14	2	9	3		58	5	4
20 mm. Quad. Battery	7	73	151	163	59	15	4		12		59	6	4
Heavy AA. Column	2	10	56	65	3	1	2				28	2	
TOTALS	39	403	908	1051	241	93	17	30	18	12	339	38	12

*Replaced by a 9 gun 3.7 cm. AA. battery in some battalions.

The 88 in action.

"Flaming Onion" shells being loaded into an 88.

A Zünderstell maschine 18 in use. One round is in the process of being set while another is being inserted by the No. 7.

These gunners are on duty in a coastal defence battery in January 1941. Note the overalls and heavy duty gloves. ▼

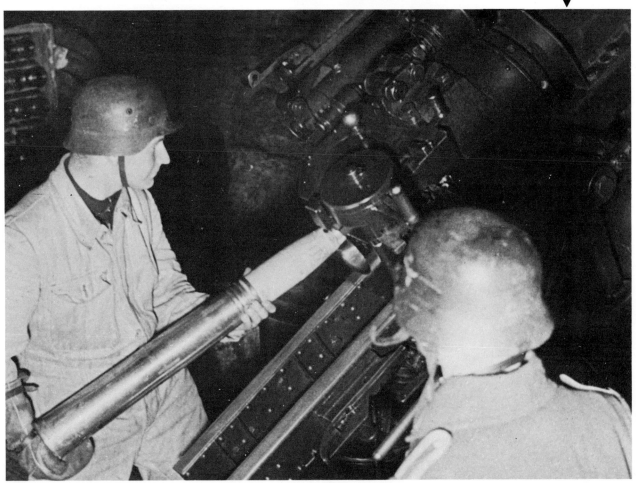

*8.8cm Flak 18 auf
Selbsfahrlafette
Zugkraftwagen 12t in action in
France 1940. (Courtesy:
Major James W. Loop.)*

*The crew of a Flak 36 carrying
out gun drill in an emplacement
in Greece.* ▼

First Published in 1976 by
Profile Publications Limited,
Windsor, Berkshire, England.

Printed in England by Edwin Snell printers, Yeovil, Somerset.

weight 10.00kg/(22.05lb), complete round weight 23.00kg(50.72lb).

This was a conventional piercing shell with penetrating and ballistic caps, and two iron driving bands each 11.4mm(0.45in) wide. It carried the usual small bursting charge, a base fuze and a tracer. The propelling charge was 6.83kg(15.06lb) of Gudol R P.

8.8cm Pzgr Patr 39/43: fuzed Bd Z 5127, projectile weight 10.16kg(22.40lb), complete round weight 23.35kg(51.49lb).

The original Pzgr 39–1 was found to be inaccurate when fired from worn guns, and so its use was eventually restricted to guns whose barrels had fired less than 500 rounds. To replace it, a new projectile was produced with heavier driving bands 16.5mm(0.65in) wide. In every other respect this round was the same as the Pzgr 39–1.

8.8cm Pzgr Patr 40: projectile weight 7.30kg (16.10lb).

This was a full-calibre tungsten-cored shot, similar to the Pzgr 40 shot used with the 7.5cm PAK 40. Few were made (since the tungsten ban came into force before stocks could be built up) and owing to this no data on the propelling charge or the complete round weight are available.

8.8cm Sprgr Patr L/4.7: fuzed AZ 23/28, projectile weight 9.40kg(20.73lb), complete round weight 19.30kg(42.56lb).

This was the original high explosive round, the shell of which came from the Flak 41. It was of conventional type, impact fuzed and carried two FES driving bands each 11.4mm(0.45in) wide. The propelling charge was 3.40kg(7.50lb) of Gudol R P.

8.8cm Sprgr Patr 43: fuzed AZ 23/28, projectile weight 9.40kg(20.73lb), complete round weight 19.30kg(42.56lb).

In the same way that the Pzgr 39–1 developed instability in a worn gun, so did the original high explosive shell; it was redesigned to use two FES driving bands each 17.8mm(0.70in) wide. Apart from this feature the Sprgr 43 was the same as the Sprgr L/4.7.

8.8cm Gr Patr 39 H1: fuzed AZ 38, projectile weight 7.65kg(16.87lb), complete round weight 16.00kg(35.28lb).

This was a hollow charge shell of the usual type. Although available to the anti-tank gun it was more commonly used by the tank guns of the family. This version had a shell with two 11.4mm (0.45in) driving bands of sintered iron. The propelling charge was 1.70kg(3.75lb) of Gudol R P.

8.8cm Gr Patr 39/43 H1: fuzed AZ 38, projectile weight 7.65kg(16.87lb), complete round weight 16.00kg(35.28lb).

This was an improved round differing, as with the other types, only in having the 17.8mm(0.70in) FES driving bands. The remainder of the data was the same. The hollow charge projectiles achieved a muzzle velocity of 600mps(1968fps), and penetration at 1000m was quoted as 90mm (3.54in) of plate at a 30° impact angle.

Primer
The electric primer C/22 was standard.

Case Identification Number: 6388.

8·8cm Panzerabwehrkanone 43/41

8·8cm Pak 43/41 (Nierstein)

War waits not upon manufacturers, and in 1943 the situation in Russia urgently demanded more anti-tank guns. Since the barrels of the PAK 43 were relatively easy to make, but the carriage manufacture was lagging, a temporary expedient was produced. The PAK 41 barrel was fitted with a horizontal sliding block breech mechanism resembling that of the 7.5cm PAK 40 and the semi-automatic gear was a simplified version of that used on the PAK 43. The carriage was a collection of suitably modified stock components; the trail legs came from the 10.5cm le FH 18, the wheels were taken from the 15cm s FH and the saddle was a steel-plate fabrication that tied everything together. A serious fault was the absence of articulation in the suspension, which meant that the gun rested on four points of contact when firing. In spite of all this it was an effective weapon and it is on record that one knocked out six T34 tanks at a range of 3500m (3828yd). Another report stated that a T34, attacked from the rear at a range of 600m (656yd), had the engine block flung out for a distance of 5m(16.41ft) and the cupola lid landed 15m(49.22ft) away. But the PAK 43/41's weight and awkwardness were notorious, and it was nicknamed Scheuntor ('barndoor') by the troops who had to use it.

An 8.8cm PAK 43/41 on display at Aberdeen Proving Ground.

Breech and sights of the 8.8cm PAK 43/41.

Side view of the 7.5cm PAK 40.

A 7.5cm PAK 40 on show at Aberdeen Proving Ground.

The 5cm PAK 38 in the travelling position.

diameter as the head in order to leave sufficient space around the muzzle stick for the tail to pass over the gun's muzzle brake. The warhead contained 2.33kg(5.14lb) of cyclonite/TNT and the special cartridge carried a charge of 770gm (27.15oz/1.70lb) of Ngl R P. It was capable of

commended maximum engagement range was 150m(165yd).

Primer
The percussion primer C/13nA was standard.

rifled gun. The sealing ring at the rear was free to rotate with the rifling, and the rear portion of the shell body carried six fins connected to a plunger that fitted tightly into a cylinder in the body. A fine hole was drilled through the plunger to give access to the cylinder. When fired, propellant gas passed through the hole and filled the cylinder's free space with gas at chamber pressure —about 3150kg/cm^2(20ton/in^2). Nothing happened in the bore (since the same pressure existed outside the piston), but when the shell left the muzzle and entered an area of atmospheric pressure— about 7.03kg/cm^2(14.7lb/in^2)—the gas in the cylinder, unable to escape quickly through the smallbore hole, expanded and forced the plunger out: this, by means of the connexion, swung the fins out into the airstream. A spring-catch on the plunger ensured that, when the gas pressure was exhausted, the fins were locked in the open position.

No details of performance are known. A report

staff, however, Hitler had authorised the manufacture of 40000 shells, the parts for which were being made at seven different factories; final assembly was the task of DWM at Lübeck. But, in spite of all this, development was never successfully completed.

Primer
The percussion primer C/12nA was standard.
Case Identification Number
6340. The cartridge case used with this equipment was 715mm(28.15in) long and stamped 7.5CM PAK 40 6340 on the base, but a number of rounds were assembled with a case 667mm(26.26in) long and stamped 7.5CM PAK 44 RH 6340 ST on the base. The PAK 44 was a different weapon whose development failed to bear fruit, as will be seen later. Cartridge cases which had been produced for this gun were then used up, slightly modified as necessary, in the PAK 40 and in the 7.62cm PAK 36(r) guns. The correct nomenclature of the